JOSSEY-BASS™
A Wiley Brand

128 Recognition Ideas for Donors, Volunteers and Members

SECOND EDITION

Scott C. Stevenson, Editor

WILEY

978-1-118-69200-4   ISBN

978-1-118-70429-5   ISBN (online)

128 Recognition Ideas for Donors, Volunteers and Members — 2nd Edition

Published by

Stevenson, Inc.

P.O. Box 4528 • Sioux City, Iowa • 51104
Phone 712.239.3010 • Fax 712.239.2166
www.stevensoninc.com

128 Recognition Ideas for Donors, Volunteers and Members — 2nd Edition

128 Recognition Ideas for Donors, Volunteers and Members — 2nd Edition

Nonprofit organizations and associations exist and thrive as a result of generous donors, volunteers and members. Those supporters deserve to be recognized in special and varied ways — both publicly and privately. This manual offers great recognition ideas to both say thanks and show gratitude to donors, volunteers and members.

 ## Stewarding Volunteers: Special Ways to Say Thanks

Whether it's time for your annual volunteer recognition event or you simply want to show your appreciation on the spur of the moment, here are creative ways to thank your valuable volunteers:

- **Feed them.** Prepare a boxed dinner complete with all the dry ingredients and a recipe for an easy meal they can prepare for their family or themselves on a busy night. Wrap the box and include a clock tag saying, "Thanks for the gift of your time."

- **Write them.** When you collect volunteer time sheets, make an even exchange. Give volunteers a note of thanks from you, a staff member or from someone served by your organization.

- **Use others' words to tell them.** Creatively arrange, in a scroll format, quotes from your executive director, board members and staff about the value of volunteers. Tie printed scrolls with ribbons and present them to your volunteers.

- **Share comfort foods.** Collect recipes from each volunteer, inviting them to include personal stories about the recipe, and assemble in a cookbook format. Include a personalized thank-you from you and/or the executive director as the introduction.

- **Offer small tokens of thanks.** Give any of these small tokens with a clever message, such as:
  - ✓ A brightly colored permanent marker with a note saying, "You've made a lasting and permanent contribution to our organization!"
  - ✓ A $100,000 Grand candy bar with the note, "Just to let you know, your service is priceless to this organization."
  - ✓ A ruler/tape measure with the message, "It's easy to measure the difference you've made in our organization — you're amazing!"
  - ✓ A shirt with a note, "We know you'd give the shirt off your back… so here's an extra one for the next time you give your all."
  - ✓ A bottle of sparkling apple juice with the message, "Cheers to a super volunteer!"

 ## Celebrate Your New Members

For years, members of the Minnesota Lake Lions (Minnesota Lake, MN) have been dedicated to their goal: helping persons with sight and hearing impairments.

Tradition and ceremony are a large part of the success of organizations like the Lions. For this organization of just 30, gaining new members is cause for celebration.

When new members join and officers are elected, the group's district governor conducts an induction ceremony.

"This is a formal setting where the officers and members are recognized and applauded," says Mike Rasmusson, Minnesota Lake Lion of the Year.

Rasmusson cites three benefits to conducting ceremonies to honor officers and new members:

- The new members feel a sense of commitment and take an oath affirming their commitment to the organization.

- The sponsoring member offers a pin to the new members as a sign of their commitment and a reminder of the group's goals.

- Existing members feel a renewed sense of commitment in leading the new members and to the organization's goals.

A new member ceremony does not require lengthy planning or great cost to the organization, but can reap much in the way of commitment by a new member. Maybe it's time to celebrate new members with a ceremony at your organization.

Source: Mike Rasmusson, Lion of the Year, Minnesota Lake Lions, Minnesota Lake, MN. Phone (507) 362-3611.
E-mail: mrasmusson@valleybank.net

3 Create Donor Photo Books

For a unique major donor gift, create a book with photos of a special event, building project or constituents using your facilities and/or programs.

For instance, a hardcover, 20-page, 8-1/2 X 11-inch book from Shutterfly (www.shutterfly.com) costs under $30.

"You could use the same photos for each book, but personalize the text for each donor," says Allie Smith, donor relations coordinator, Oregon Food Bank (Portland, OR). "With one click, you could also create a softcover 5 X 7-inch version of the same book for $10 to $15."

For a more personal connection, leave space next to each photo for clients to write personal messages.

Additional photo book websites:

✓ www.Kodakgallery.com — Click "Shop," then "Photo Books"

✓ www.Lulu.com — Click "Publish," then "Photo Books"

✓ www.mypublisher.com

✓ www.picaboo.com

✓ www.photobookmemories.com

Source: Allie Smith, Donor Relations Coordinator, Oregon Food Bank, Portland, OR. Phone (503) 282-0555, ext. 283. E-mail: Asmith@oregonfoodbank.org

4 Tailor Recognition To Senior Volunteers

While the age groups of people who volunteer are becoming more diverse, many organizations still rely on seniors.

Here are ideas for tailoring volunteer recognition to seniors:

- Hold the recognition ceremony during the day since some seniors may not feel comfortable traveling at night. The event can be made into a brunch, lunch or early afternoon light meal.

- Cater the music, food and games of your recognition event to your seniors' tastes. Ask for feedback after each event on what the senior volunteers liked and disliked.

- Make sure every volunteer gets a prize or gift. Little prizes will mean more than the chance to win two or three big ones.

- Give discounts for classes or memberships at the local senior center as recognition gifts.

- Partner with a local grocery store and ask them to offer your senior volunteers 10 percent off on a certain day.

- Give senior volunteers reserved parking spaces that are within close walking distance to the front doors.

5 Steward Donors Year-round

Does your brand-new, $20 donor expect a thank-you call from your CEO?

That's what Christina Thrun, development and marketing director, Big Brothers Big Sisters Northwestern Wisconsin (Eau Claire, WI), wants to know.

You see, her donors don't expect it — but they get it, thanks to stewardship efforts that have taken on a whole new level for the organization.

"Stewardship is more than a thank-you card," she says. "It's everything that you do (throughout the year) that goes above and beyond what the donor expects."

She shares other stewardship steps from the organization's development plan:

✓ Any new donor, no matter how much they give, receives a personal thank-you call from the CEO. New significant donors are offered a meeting with organization staff, at their own office, to hear about the direct impact their gift is making.

✓ Donors receive hand-made cards from the organization's matches (adult volunteers, or "bigs," and their assigned young clients, or "littles"). Staff provides examples of what to write so the donors receive cards that are actually suitable for the intended purpose. The bigs and littles are asked to work on these cards at quarterly big/little events.

✓ Starting in January 2010, donors received thank-you calls from bigs and littles during a phone thank-a-thon tied to National Mentoring Month. Matches were asked to donate 90 minutes of their time, visiting the organization's offices to make calls. Scripts, pizza and soda were provided.

Source: Christina Thrun, Development and Marketing Director, Big Brothers Big Sisters Northwestern Wisconsin, Eau Claire, WI. Phone (715) 835-0161. E-mail: Christina.Thrun@bbbs.org

Recognize Volunteers Every Step of the Way

At the Seattle Aquarium (Seattle, WA) volunteers are not only recognized for years of service, but hours of service.

Each and every milestone of service is rewarded with a variety of perks and the listing of the volunteer's name in the organization's newsletter, the All Wet Gazette.

"Some volunteers are with us for years, but can only give a few hours, while others can give a lot of hours but may not serve more than five or 10 years — we recognize both hours and years served," says Sue Donohue Smith, guest experience manager.

At the aquarium, volunteers serving 100, 250, 500, 1,000 and every 1,000 hours after receive a certificate in appreciation of their efforts and recognition in the newsletter.

In addition, volunteers who have reached their first 100 hours of service receive a patch for their uniform. They then receive rockers, which are smaller patches that fit around the large patch that signify different jobs, every five years of service and every 1,000 hours of service. Also, all volunteers receive pins for every year of service, with each pin portraying a different animal.

All volunteers receive the monthly newsletter and Weekly Critter News publications as a perk, as well as invitations to socials and picnics including the Dive Social and Exotic Team picnic.

"By recognizing volunteers at the small levels, you set them up to stay with you."

Volunteers are also invited to staff meetings to instill their importance to the organization, and receive one entrance ticket for every 25 hours served, plus a free family membership after six months of service.

"By recognizing volunteers at the small levels, you set them up to stay with you," says Donohue Smith. "The bottom line is that volunteers at the Seattle Aquarium know they are important and critical to our success. They learn this on day one, and it is reinforced to them constantly."

Follow the lead of the Seattle Aquarium, recognize your volunteers at every milestone no matter how big or small.

Source: Sue Donohue Smith, Guest Experience Manager, Seattle Aquarium, Seattle, WA. Phone (206) 399-7033. E-mail: sue.donohue-smith@seattle.gov

 ## Appropriate Gifts to Say Thanks to Foundations

Q. We would like to thank our foundation donors for their recent grants to our organization. What type of gifts do foundations prefer to receive?

"Frequently, development-oriented people react to foundation giving with an individual giving mindset rather than a foundation mindset. Unless it's a small family foundation — which is often just a vehicle by which individuals are doing their personal giving — this doesn't work. At my first foundation relations job, as early as the interview process it became apparent to me that the top folks in development did not understand that foundation giving works differently than individual giving. It's important to match the mode of thanks to the motivation for giving — individuals like personal recognition, corporations like visibility and foundations like knowing they've done good. A sincere letter of thanks and a press release, which you have cleared with the foundation, usually takes care of that!"

— Deborah S. Koch, Director of Grants, Springfield Technical Community College (Springfield, MA)

"It depends on the foundation, of course. Recently, we did something that worked well for one of our major foundation donors. The foundation had been giving a yearly grant to be used for scholarships for 28 years. We contacted all of the previous student recipients and asked them to write a letter

of thanks to the foundation. About 20 students responded with wonderful letters of where they are now and how the scholarship helped them achieve their goals. We then put the letters together with a recent picture and their yearbook picture in a Snapfish photo book. The foundation loved it! We also kept a copy for the development office and use it when we meet with prospective donors to show the impact of scholarships on our students."

— Suzanne Libenson, Director of Foundation Relations and Government Funding, Holy Family University (Philadelphia, PA)

"Because we're a small, private institution, we try not to be too extravagant when it comes to donor recognition. All donors, including foundation donors, receive an official thank-you letter from our president. I also handwrite a note to our foundation donors and call them if I happen to know someone at the foundation. If the grant is for student scholarships, students will also write thank-you letters to the foundation. Foundation donors are also recognized on our outdoor donor recognition wall, on giving society plaques in our administration building and in the college's online annual honor roll of donors."

— Cindy C. Godwin, Director of Development, Meredith College (Raleigh, NC)

8 Who Were Your Founding Board Members?

Has your organization been around awhile? Here's an idea to give credit to and celebrate its founders:

Identify the descendents of founding board members and invite them — after thorough cultivation — to make a naming gift in honor of their ancestors. Give this approach even more significance by timing it to a significant milestone in your organization's history.

9 Donor Recognition Idea

Have you ever considered using your organization's board meetings as a way to recognize key donors' generous gifts?

Make a point to invite recent donors to be introduced and perhaps make a brief address at each meeting. Doing so provides a special kind of donor recognition and also emphasizes the importance of principal giving among board members and staff.

10 Personalization Makes Volunteer Recognition Memorable

Volunteers play a crucial role in the success of many organizations and businesses, and rightly so. After all, you don't want your volunteers' efforts to go unnoticed. But what can you do to make your recognition a memorable event?

Jona Alborn, psychosocial coordinator, Liberty Hospice Services (Raeford, NC), found a way to express her appreciation that was so memorable, volunteers were talking about it a full year after the event.

The memorable recognition took place during National Volunteer Week 2007, when Alborn was volunteer coordinator at Liberty Hospice. To thank her volunteers, she took them out to dinner. Following dinner she presented them with a certificate and award. Sounds pretty run-of-the-mill, right?

Well, this wasn't just any award. Each of her 15 volunteers received a special gift personally chosen for the way it directly correlated to the service he or she provided.

The awards included:

- A tiara for the volunteer with the most hours in 2007. She was crowned Queen of Volunteer Hours.
- A silver sheriff's badge for the volunteer who watched Audie Murphy westerns twice a week with one of the hospice patients.
- A Golden Spoon Award for the aunt-and-niece team that fed patients at a nursing facility.
- Iris bulbs for the gardening volunteer who took plants to the patient he visited.

"We've given them other things throughout the years," Alborn says, "but this is what they are still talking about."

Another plus? The gifts were only $1 to $3 each at a local dollar store. "They were very inexpensive novelty items," Alborn says. But, these gifts are "special treasures to them yet today."

Why were these awards such a hit? Because Alborn specially selected each one for the individual volunteer.

"What they give to us, what they give to the patients is so much energy and life and special experiences," she says. "I was just glad to give something back to them as individuals."

Alborn says the personalization process was not time consuming. In fact, she says, she spent less than two hours browsing the store to find the right items.

The key to such a recognition program, she says, is knowing your volunteers.

When Alborn was a volunteer coordinator, she says, she tried to develop a relationship with each volunteer. One way she did this was by making an effort to call them to say, "Hi," rather than just when she needed their assistance. Through these friendly conversations, she grew to know the volunteers as more than just names, but as individuals, each with a unique reason for lending his/her time and talents to the worthwhile cause.

So how did Alborn top the 2007 event t? For the 2008 National Volunteer Week, she and her staff presented volunteers with T-shirts and entertained them with a magic show.

Source: Jona Alborn, Psychosocial Coordinator, Liberty Hospice Services, Raeford, NC. Phone (910) 584-9287.
E-mail: jalborn@libertyhomecare.com.
Website: www.libertyhomecare.com

Match Gifts, Personalities

No matter what your cause may be, you can find gifts that say thanks in a personal way, just by getting to know your volunteers a little bit better.

Whether by phone or personal visit, check in with volunteers as regularly as possible. Along with asking them how their volunteer experience is, ask them a little about what they do outside of your organization, as well.

Then put this knowledge to work to match a gift with the individual.

An avid reader who volunteers for the animal shelter may love a set of books by author/veterinarian James Herriot, while the green thumb who donates hours to your children's program would surely enjoy a pot of whimsical plants such as lamb's ears and bunny-tail grasses.

11 Calendar Thanks Donors, Recognizes Constituents

Some promotional tools do double duty.

For example, staff with James Madison University's Office of Advancement (Harrisonburg, VA) developed the "Be the Change" calendar to coincide with the university's "Be the Change" campaign, launched in 2006. The calendar celebrates persons making a difference while thanking donors.

"The calendar promotes the university's alumni, faculty and students who are making a difference in the world," says Theresa Lind, events coordinator. "It illuminates how these people arm themselves with the power of knowledge, as Madison did, to change the world for the better."

Distributed since the campaign's launch, the 4 1/2 X 5 1/2-inch calendars are given at the university's scholarship luncheon, regional campaign events and given to various donors by development officers, alumni, faculty and staff.

Persons wishing to nominate someone for the calendar can complete a nomination form online (www.jmu.edu/bethechange) or with a calendar insert. Nominations must explain how the person has made a difference, how he/she made a contribution to "Be the Change," plus the nominee's name, address and affiliation to the university.

A committee in the communications, marketing and public affairs office reviews nominations and selects persons to appear on the calendar pages.

Source: Theresa Lind, Events Coordinator, James Madison University, Harrisburg, VA.
Phone (540) 568-8867. E-mail: lindtl@jmu.edu

12 Get the Most Mileage Out of Donor Photos

When donors visit your facilities to attend a reception, see a project or program they helped fund or meet with recipients of their generosity, chances are you or your staff may take photos of the donors on site. What do you do next? Do you simply store the photos on your hard drive or in a file cabinet, never to be seen again?

Here are some options for making the best use of donor photos:

✓ Send a photo of the donor to the donor along with a personal note of gratitude.

✓ If the donor's gift helped a specific person (e.g., scholarship recipient, patient), send that person a photo with a note saying, "Perhaps you will be able to assist someone one day just as this person assisted you."

✓ Keep a photo in the donor's file so staff can identify donors when they visit again.

✓ Develop a feature story to accompany each photo that can be pitched to the media. Maintain an up-to-date file of feature possibilities.

✓ Maintain a yearly photo album in your lobby or a wall display that depicts your nonprofit's ties to its many donors.

13 Present Retiring Volunteers With Book of Memories

When you have volunteers retiring after a long period of service, provide them with a going-away gift they will genuinely treasure. One idea? A scrapbook of their personal involvement with your organization over the years.

To prepare for that down-the-road occasion:

✓ Take photos of volunteers in action and keep a copy in each volunteer's file.

✓ When you do any sort of story about a volunteer, keep a copy of it.

✓ Maintain an ongoing list of all of the projects in which each volunteer participated during his/her tenure with your organization.

✓ Solicit and save testimonials from people whose lives were touched by volunteers.

When a volunteer departs your organization, you will have a file of materials that can be assembled into a meaningful scrapbook and presented at a farewell event. Save room for fellow volunteers, clients and employees to write personal messages.

Applaud Those Who Make Major Gifts Beyond Your Charity

It's all over the local news. An individual in your community has just made a transforming major gift to a charity — just not yours.

Should you do anything about it? After all, the gift has nothing to do with your organization. Or does it? Think about it. Whenever someone makes a major gift to any charity, that sends a tremendously positive message to others about the good and importance of philanthropy. Any major gift creates a positive ripple effect that not only raises awareness about philanthropy, but also spurs others to consider what they might one day do — including your own board members and existing donors.

Rather than doing nothing, why not write a letter of praise to the donor commending his/her generosity to the other charity? In fact, send a copy of your letter to an official with the other charity. At right is an example of a letter that illustrates how to do this in good taste.

```
Dear [Donor]:

I want to be among those in our community to praise you
for the recent gift you made to [XYZ Charity]. I know your
generosity will have a tremendously positive impact on
those served by this deserving agency.

I also want to point out that your gift has ramifications
that go even beyond the charity to which you have
contributed. Whenever someone makes a financial
contribution of this magnitude — one that has a
transforming impact on an organization's mission — it
creates a new level of awareness among others who have the
capability of making significant gifts. It starts others
thinking, "Maybe I should give thought to a gift."

[Donor], not only have you helped [XYZ Charity] in an
unprecedented way, you have helped all deserving causes
through this act of generosity. You have raised the
philanthropic bar in our community and throughout this
region.

Thank you on behalf of all nonprofit organizations
throughout this area! You have helped pave the way for
increased giving that will benefit all of us and those we
serve.

Respectfully

[Your Name]

Cc: [CEO, XYZ Charity]
```

 Displays That Recognize Volunteers' Contributions

Go beyond the traditional bulletin board with these ways to call attention to volunteers' contributions to your cause:

- **Public Video Presentation.** Create a permanent lobby display that can serve a variety of purposes to build your volunteer program. Use a DVD player to share a CD of volunteers at work, home and at volunteer duties.

- **Interactive Virtual Display.** Build a computer kiosk with a touch screen where visitors can select a topic and view a biographical sketch of volunteers, including facts and figures related to the impact they have on your organization. Provide a screen or post information of whom to contact to become a volunteer.

- **Free Media.** Develop a partnership with local media outlets where you can submit a brief press release or public service announcement each month to announce a special volunteer. In return, recognize the media outlet as a sponsor of one of your community betterment projects.

- **Volunteer Scrapbook.** Even if your budget is small, you can create a scrapbook for every important volunteer you want to honor. Start one honoring another person each month, quarter or year, as budget and time allow (this would be an ideal project for a crafty volunteer). Ask friends and family for photos of milestones, including shots of the person volunteering. Use clippings, mementoes and certificates. Leave the book on display for visitors, staff and clients to enjoy before the honoree takes it home.

- **Multipurpose Display.** On a writing table or desk in your reception area, place a framed photo of a volunteer with the caption, "Why I Volunteer." Include personalized flyers in which the subject answers the question, along with information on where the person volunteers. Include a form to fill out to receive more information about volunteering, or have pens and a drop box so persons can complete the form on site. Change the display and story monthly.

16 Match-of-the-month Cards Recognize Members

Recognizing your most active members can pay off in many ways.

Development staff with Big Brothers Big Sisters of Greater Miami (Miami, FL) send high-end donors Match-of-the-month cards that celebrate a specific adult/child match and showcase the organization's purpose, says Ryan Roth, development manager.

The card front features a photo of the "big" adult member and "little" child member participating in the mentoring program. Inside is a story of the benefits of their relationship written by the adult member. On the back is an inspirational quote on mentoring.

Through the program, which is about a year old, 150 full-color cards are mailed to major contributors each month. To add a personal touch, cards are signed by the CEO, vice president of development, development manager and vice president of programs.

"We send these to our high-end donors so they can see monthly how their dollars are being put to good use," Roth says. "A major component of my job is stewardship, and this is one of the many ways we thank our donors, along with thank-a-thon campaigns, donor surveys, personal phone calls and recognition at events."

The cards are planned about one month in advance.

"Each month, one of our match support persons (who help guide the mentoring relationships) is responsible for providing a match to feature on the cards that they feel has been truly helped because of the one-on-one relationship we provide," he says.

The cards have become a marketing tool to help recruit new members as well, says Roth, noting that many donors keep them on their desks at work, where people ask about them and learn about getting involved in the organization.

"Feedback has been great," he says. "We receive e-mails and phone calls from donors saying they appreciate us taking the time to send out the cards. We also get comments at events."

Source: Ryan Roth, Development Manager, Big Brothers Big Sisters of Greater Miami, Miami, FL. Phone (305) 644-0066. E-mail: rroth@bbbsmiami.org

---

17 Host an Annual Memorial Event for Employees, Constituents

To honor the memory of those close to your organization — donors, volunteers, employees, board members and others — why not host an annual memorial event that recognizes those who have died during the past year?

Invite loved ones of persons who have passed away, as well as the public, to an hour-long service that pays tribute to persons who had a connection to your organization.

Such an annual service might include:

✓ Asking the family and friends of each individual to stand and be recognized.

✓ A printed program listing those who have died during the past year along with a brief bio of their lives and affiliation with your organization.

✓ A permanent wall display or memorial book to honor those who have been memorialized in past years.

An annual service such as this shows respect for these individuals' contributions and emphasizes the fact that they were an important part of your nonprofit's extended family.

---

18 Show Appreciation With Personal Calls to Say Thanks

Looking for a fresh way to say thanks to your volunteers?

Whether you do so at your organization's recognition ceremony during National Volunteer Week or simply recognize their efforts for no other reason than to say thank you, try this idea used by the volunteer department of Seacoast Hospice (Exeter, NH):

Janet Prescott, associate director of community relations and development, says in honor of National Volunteer Week they decided to take a nontraditional approach to show their appreciation.

"Instead of planning yet another event, which most volunteers are too busy to attend, we divided up our list of more than 300 volunteers among 15 of our staff members, including our CEO," Prescott says. "We then asked them to place a simple call to thank the volunteers.

"The volunteers loved getting the thank-you calls, even if the messages were left on their answering machines. For once, we weren't calling to ask them to do something for us. We were simply saying, 'Thank you, we appreciate everything you do!'"

Source: Janet Prescott, Associate Director of Community Relations and Development, Seacoast Hospice, Exeter, NH. Phone (603) 778-7391. E-mail: jprescott@seacoasthospice.org

19   Decide On Donor Recognition Prior to Capital Campaign

When someone makes a significant gift, how do you recognize and celebrate that donor's generosity?

One option worth considering is purchasing naming plaques for buildings, rooms, equipment or other items purchased with donors' major gifts.

Ideally, determine exact methods of donor recognition during the planning phase of your capital campaign, as doing so allows you to best budget for such well-deserved recognition. And if you are mid-campaign, take time to regroup and set recognition standards, taking into account gifts received to date.

To create appropriate recognition for your campaign, answer these questions:

1. What form of recognition will be given to each publicized naming gift opportunity — plaques with individual donors' names, a plaque that lists all major donors?

2. Will the various forms of recognition have any degree of consistency even though some donors will contribute much more than others?

3. How much are we prepared to spend for various forms of donor recognition?

4. Will the type of recognition given be appropriate for the gift size?

5. Where will each plaque be placed?

6. In addition to permanent recognition at our facility, will the donor receive some token of appreciation to display at home or work?

7. Will we want to coordinate a celebration, open house or other event to publicly thank all donors at the campaign's conclusion? How much are we willing to spend for that?

8. Is there a minimum gift amount for which donors will receive special recognition?

9. What process will be followed to ensure donors are selecting the name or names they want included along with proper spelling?

Answers to these and other questions will help ensure donors are appropriately recognized and associated recognition costs are covered.

 20   Special Volunteers Deserve Special Recognition

Honoring volunteers doesn't require an expensive trophy or engraved plaque. Here are ideas for true gifts of the heart that will be treasured by your dedicated supporters:

- **Name a special day for him/her.** Publicize throughout your organization that it's "Jane Jones Day." Print posters and adhesive lapel labels for staff to wear with Jane's picture to prompt visitors to ask who she is and why she is so important.

- **Tell the media about your volunteer.** Newspapers and local radio and public-access TV programs frequently look for vibrant volunteers as feature subjects. Identify a solid human-interest angle (e.g., fulfillment of 1,000 volunteer hours or three generations of volunteers) and send a news release to local media.

- **Hold a potluck dinner or picnic in his/her honor.** Choose a festive setting and ask fellow volunteers to make a favorite dish and recipe for a "Jane Feeds Our Hearts and Souls" cookbook she can enjoy and pass on to future generations.

- **Create a surprise memory book.** Find a large, attractive scrapbook and give as many volunteers as possible a page to personalize and decorate with messages, photos and favorite stories about your valued friend. For appearance consistency, provide a small craft table with all supplies needed and ask contributors to complete their page at your headquarters.

- **Plant a tree or make a similar green gesture.** Trees, rosebushes and other lasting plants can be an affordable and ecologically friendly way to honor your volunteer. If your organization doesn't have a permanent spot for a tree to grow, you can have it delivered to the volunteer's home after making inquiries about what he/she might like to plant on his/her own property.

- **Collect and give favorite gift certificates.** Find a theme and activities the volunteer enjoys, like a good book and cup of coffee or tea. Put an assortment of gift cards in a colorful basket with related useful items like a personalized ceramic mug and small bottles of flavored syrups or sweeteners.

21 Want to Thank and Recognize Members? Take Out an Ad!

Thanking members for their patronage can be a simple process — as simple as taking out an ad in your local newspaper, says Katie DiMaria, executive director, Niles Chamber of Commerce (Niles, IL).

In conjunction with Chamber of Commerce week occurring the second week of September, the Niles Chamber of Commerce takes out a two-page, center-spread ad in the local saturation newspaper, which goes to every home and business in Niles, DiMaria says. The ad lists all 475 chamber members by anniversary date, with some members going back as far as 35 years with the chamber. The banner of the ad thanks the members for their support of the chamber and encourages readers to shop locally.

So what is accomplished with such an ad? The executive director says the ad offers local business owners recognition and visibility for their business while allowing the chamber to show support of its members.

Plus, shoppers are encouraged to keep their business in town.

"The ad is very well-received," says DiMaria, noting that any time they can provide an additional service such as this to members, that they don't pay extra for, is a benefit. "It also helps us to show our appreciation and helps promote their business."

As an added touch, DiMaria arranges to have chamber ambassadors and board members hand-deliver the special issue of the paper to members.

Source: Katie DiMaria, Executive Director, Niles Chamber of Commerce, Niles, IL. Phone (847) 268-8180.
E-mail: Katie@nileschamber.com

22 Offer Volunteer Jamboree Filled With Education and Fun

Want to wow your volunteers at your annual appreciation event? Go beyond the typical thank-you luncheon to offer a day of fun, networking, camaraderie and education.

Staff with the Salt Lake County Office of Volunteer Program Services (Salt Lake City, UT) invited members to the first-ever, day-long jamboree of educational workshops in 2008, says Virginia Lee, volunteer program manager.

The event was a huge success, drawing some 200 volunteers to Salt Lake County's Free Wheeler Historic Farm, says Lee. Costs were kept low (around $1,500, including lunch) thanks to the donated venue as well as speakers donating their services.

Kicking off the day was the keynote address, "Do I Care About Me?" that touched on personal health issues as well as maintaining motivation in a volunteer setting.

Workshops covered topics in line with both volunteer efforts and the mayor's goals for the county, Lee says, including: connecting with county government; disaster planning; customer service; teamwork; and recycling.

Source: Virginia Lee, Volunteer Program Manager, Salt Lake County Office of Volunteer Program Services, Salt Lake City, UT. Phone (801) 468-2185. E-mail: vlee@slco.org

23 Honor Top Supporters With a Recognition Award

Missouri State University already offered several awards for academic giving, employee support and the like. Why did university officials need another?

To recognize a very important constituency, Brent Dunn, vice president of university of advancement, says in explaining MSU's Bronze Bear Award.

"The award recognizes people who have had a major and ongoing impact on the university, whether through service, financial support or both," Dunn says. "It honors a lifetime of service."

Recipients are endorsed by the university administrative council, faculty senate, staff senate and student government association before being approved by the board of governors. Recipients are presented with a framed resolution and 18-inch, 45-pound bronze bear statuette at winter commencement proceedings and invited to address the graduating class.

Working to maximize recognition for both the recipients and the university, officials publicize both the Board of Governors' approval in October and at the December presentation ceremony.

Dunn says the award not only honors past supporters, it inspires new ones.

"Bronze Bear recipients include past university presidents, former members of the Board of Governors and nationally recognized philanthropists. It's a very prestigious group," he says. "Winning an award is not what moves people to serve, but it does establish a great level of support that others might strive to emulate."

Source: Brent Dunn, Vice President for University Advancement, Missouri State University, Springfield, MO. Phone (417) 836-6666. E-mail: brentdunn@missouristate.edu

24 Simple Thank You is an Effective Tool in Donor Stewardship

Is your advancement office looking for a simple yet effective way to show donors your appreciation? How about saying thank you?

Those two powerful little words, combined with the message "We couldn't have done it without you," grace the front of a postcard that goes to all donors to Simmons College (Boston, MA) at the end of each fiscal year.

Katie Miller, assistant director, donor relations, says they mailed 8,000 of the 7 X 5-inch postcards at the end of the 2006-2007 fiscal year. They have used the simple-yet-effective communications tools since 2004 as one small piece of an advancement effort that involves a 60-person staff.

"The purpose of these postcards is a part of our overall stewardship strategy to increase donors," Miller says. "We make a real effort to show the specific impact each gift has upon the college."

The back of the postcard briefly mentions how many supporters gave, how much was donated and how those funds were used. In 2006-2007 more than 7,500 alumni, parents and friends gave gifts totaling nearly $9.8 million,

Miller says.

To show this past year's donors how their contributions impacted Simmons, the advancement office included these three points on the postcard:

1. The gifts helped to award more than $19 million in scholarships and other financial aid to 2,338 students.

2. Donations provided study-abroad opportunities to more than 200 students in countries such as South Africa, Costa Rica, India, Spain and Thailand.

3. Gifts helped complete renovation of Beatley Library, which nearly doubled in size to include 14 group study rooms, 108 computer carrels and 40 laptops students can check out.

With the postcard donors receive a tri-fold, full-color calendar with a brief note of appreciation and best wishes for the new year from the vice president of advancement.

Source: Katie Miller, Assistant Director, Donor Relations, Office of Advancement, Simmons College, Boston, MA.

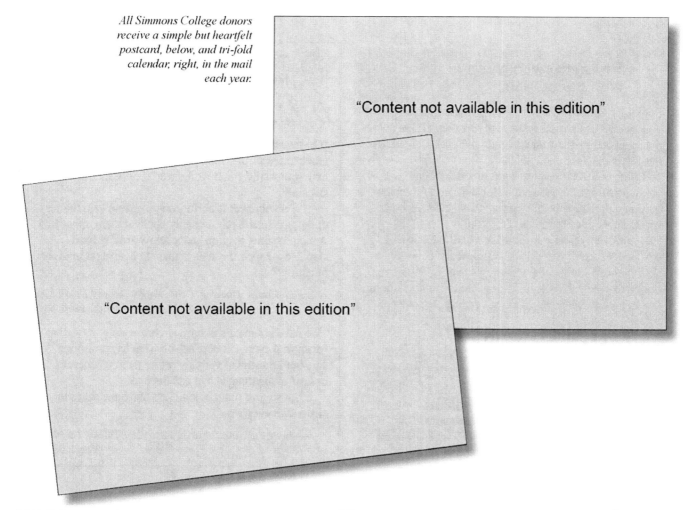

All Simmons College donors receive a simple but heartfelt postcard, below, and tri-fold calendar, right, in the mail each year.

"Content not available in this edition"

"Content not available in this edition"

25 Recognizing Your Top Donor

Q. What do you do to recognize your most significant donor in a significant way?"

"At the American Diabetes Association and with our Research Foundation, we have a standard set of recognition opportunities (personal tours during our scientific sessions, names in annual reports and ads in our consumer publication, Diabetes Forecast). But what makes our stewardship unique is that our stewardship director will discuss with our staff member and our donor ways that are meaningful to him or her. For example, we don't own a building, but we do have research grants that can be named in honor of the donor. Then each time the researcher is published, we give the donor copies of the article. We will also arrange personal lab tours at private gatherings for the donor and the scientists."

— Elly Brtva, Managing Director of Individual Gifts, American Diabetes Association (Alexandria, VA)

"This past year, the office of medical development raised several endowed professorships (each professorship is a $4 million gift). At a small dinner of about 50 people hosted by the dean of the medical school, we recognize the donor and the faculty who will be the chair holder. The donor and faculty member each receives a professorship medal and Stanford chair in addition to professionally designed photo albums commemorating the evening."

— Lorraine Alexander, Senior Director of Development, Neuroscience Institute, Stanford University (Menlo Park, CA)

"The Minneapolis Institute of Arts has a long-time trustee and major benefactor who has made countless gifts over his lifetime. During the opening of our new wing, we honored him and his legacy of support by announcing a permanent art endowment in his name. His fellow trustees had contributed nearly $4 million to this art endowment as a tribute to his decades of generosity.

"As a result, the museum — and the community — now have a permanent testament to this donor's commitment to excellence in our collections."

— Joan Grathwol Olson, Director of Development, The Minneapolis Institute of Arts (Minneapolis, MN)

---

26 Recognize Volunteers With Happy Hour

Looking for new ways to recognize your organization's volunteers? Go beyond acknowledging their efforts at the usual end-of-the-year recognition dinner. Instead, try hosting happy hours.

Julie Schweer, volunteer services/marketing coordinator, I Have a Dream – Houston, says for the last 10 years, they have been honoring their volunteers with happy hours three to four times a year.

The event directly follows the end of the business day, and features food, drinks and speakers. Schweer says she works with local restaurants to donate food and offer a discounted cash bar. Prior to the event, invitations are sent out to the organization's approximately 400 active volunteers.

Schweer says the happy hours have been very well received by their volunteers. "It's definitely been successful because it builds a community among the volunteers," she says.

Source: Julie Schweer, Volunteer Services/Marketing Coordinator, I Have a Dream-Houston, Houston, TX. Phone (713) 523-7326. E-mail: volunteer@ihad-houston.org

---

27 Two Fresh Ideas for Rewarding Acts of Kindness

How do you surprise your volunteers for their acts of kindness?

"On several occasions, I have done the following, much to the surprise and pleasure of the volunteers.... It may sound silly, but it works well if done tactfully and sincerely:

"If a volunteer is performing well and is in the act of doing a superb job, I simply applaud them, literally. A nice standing ovation and a heartwarming hand clap. How happy this makes them to be caught in the act of caring!"

— Lynda Whalen, Director of Volunteer Services, Eastern New Mexico Medical Center (Roswell, NM)

"We have volunteers in our warehouse daily as well as for special events. It depends on what has transpired, for sure but I do stop to verbally praise them whenever I see or hear of anything above and beyond.

"I also give out movie tickets and bake cakes to share with everyone."

— Annie Cadirao, Volunteer Facilitator, Hawaii Foodbank (Honolulu, HI)

28 Play on Major Gift Clubs' Attraction as Status Symbol

As a donor, being associated with a major giving club can rightly bring a sense of pride.

As a development office, being aware of that element can help determine how — and to whom — to market such giving options.

The five major gift clubs offered at Clemson University (Clemson, SC) provide incentives for giving, says Ann Batson Smith, director of annual giving.

"Having gift clubs at all levels is a motivator for people to increase their gifts," says Batson Smith. "There is a certain status symbol for a donor to say they give at a major gift club level."

The annual major gift club levels offered at Clemson include:

✓ **President's Club** ($1,000 to $2,499) with 1,440 members;

✓ **Clemson Ambassadors** ($2,500 to $4,999) with 265 members;

✓ **Clemson Fellows** ($5,000 to $9,999) with 193 members;

✓ **Founders** ($10,000 to $24,999) with 200 members; and

✓ **Heritage Partners** ($25,000 or more), with 130 members.

"Donors at the major gift club level do feel there is a status associated with giving at the major giving level," Batson Smith says. "I believe they expect a certain exclusivity, so we try to send them special messages from the president or leadership groups, special invitations to major gift club events and sometimes earlier notification of campus news."

While gift clubs are great incentives to give at a higher level, Batson Smith recommends planning for increased costs associated with stewarding this group of donors while staying within Internal Revenue Service guidelines for the amount of benefits these donors receive if your organization allows 100 percent tax-deductibility for the gift.

Source: Ann Batson Smith, Director of Annual Giving, Clemson University, Clemson, SC. Phone (864) 656-5895. E-mail: annsmit@clemson.edu

29 Why Recognize Only One Volunteer Each Month?

Putting a spin on the volunteer-of-the-month tradition, Marcia Todd, coordinator of volunteer services, Alliance Community Hospital (Alliance, OH), recognizes a department of the month.

Featuring an entire department honors many of the 300 volunteers in the 172-bed hospital rather than just one, says Todd. She randomly selects a volunteer department from the hospital's 53 service areas, writes an article about its achievements and submits it to the hospital's internal newspaper, the local newspaper and hospital newsletter, along with information on how to learn more about volunteer

opportunities.

The effort helps in recruiting, Todd says. "People can see what each department does, and if it's something they're interested in, we'll get a good volunteer response."

Volunteers being honored receive gift certificates to the hospital gift shop or eatery. Both enterprises are owned by the auxiliary, and support the hospital.

Source: Marcia Todd, Coordinator of Volunteer Services, Alliance Hospital, Alliance, OH. Phone (330) 596-7821. E-mail: mtodd@achosp.org

30 Member Meeting Recognition

If your members wear name tags for events and meetings, consider this idea:

Add a star or other symbol to members' badges to recognize an accomplishment (e.g., perfect attendance, great idea of the month, contributed hours or years of service). The various symbols on an individual's badge will make them feel special while pointing out accomplishments and creating a talking point with other members.

31 Reward Volunteers By Topping Off Their Tanks

Don't let rising gas prices sink the enthusiasm of persons who may be concerned about the cost of filling up to get to their volunteer assignments.

Give $30 gas cards for volunteer recognition. Your volunteers will appreciate being able to fill their tank at no cost — and will be even more appreciative of the opportunity to lend a hand to your cause.

32 Preformatted Memory Books, Photo Albums Say Thanks

Looking for a way to thank major donors to a major event? Consider an instant photo guestbook such as the one by Adesso Albums (www.adessoalbums.com).

The guestbook, marketed on the company's website as a way to create a memory book of photos and special wishes, features spaces for Polaroid instant photos, as well as space to write special messages.

This type of thank-you gift, using any photo/memory album available in stores and online, would provide a one-of-a-kind thank-you gift to your major donors.

To get started, take photos of donors at various events throughout the year, during the five-year period of a capital campaign, etc. Next, have your president handwrite a thank you to the donor on the first page of the album. Write captions, including the dates and names of each event in the photos, throughout the album.

Another thought: Use scrapbook-type photo albums, complete with spaces for photos and journaling, for photos of clients benefiting from services provided by donors' gifts; have the clients write personal notes of thanks along with their photos.

33 Initiate Your Volunteer Hall of Fame

When it comes to managing volunteers, Iowa is definitely doing something right.

Four of Iowa's major communities — Des Moines, Cedar Rapids, Iowa City and Waterloo-Cedar Falls — rank among the top 10 cities in volunteerism efforts, according to the 2009 Volunteering in America Report by the Corporation for National and Community Service (Washington, D.C.). Iowa City boasted a rate of 49 percent of adults engaging in volunteer activity, while Iowa ranked fifth among states for volunteerism overall.

With so many Iowans volunteering, it stands to reason that Iowa takes volunteering seriously. In fact, top volunteers are recognized annually by the Iowa Volunteer Hall of Fame.

Created in 1989 by the Governor's Office for Volunteerism to honor Iowans who make extraordinary donations of volunteer service to their communities, the program is now administered by the Iowa Commission on Volunteer Service (ICVS), Des Moines, IA.

"Being inducted into the Iowa Volunteer Hall of Fame is the most prestigious state-level honor volunteers can receive (and) is truly a once-in-a-lifetime honor, since previous inductees may not be nominated again," says Jody Benz,

ICVS volunteer promotion and events coordinator. "The people selected are those who have forever changed their community, the state, the nation or the world with their volunteer service and action."

Check out the 2010 report, Volunteering in America, by the Corporation for National Community Service (Washington, D.C.), including individual state rankings, at: www.volunteeringinamerica.gov

Fellow Iowans can nominate exceptional volunteers in one of these categories:

- Individual
- Organization/Nonprofit
- Group
- Family
- Labor Union
- Business/Corporation

A ceremony in the Iowa State Capitol during the commission-sponsored annual Volunteer Awareness Day recognizes inductees, whose names are engraved on the Iowa Volunteer Hall of Fame plaque on permanent display in the Iowa Historical Building.

Source: Jody Benz, Volunteer Promotion and Events Coordinator, Iowa Commission on Volunteer Service, Des Moines, IA. Phone: (515) 725-3094. E-mail: jody.benz@iowalifechanging.com

Follow Iowa's Example to Honor Volunteers

Following Iowa's nomination criteria and eligibility standards, follow these steps to initiate a Volunteer Hall of Fame in your state — or within your organization:

❑ *Appoint a staff person to coordinate the program.* This person must be able to devote time needed, especially during the nomination/selection cycle.

❑ *Form a committee to work with the coordinator to establish a budget, timeline, nomination criteria and to select honorees.* The Iowa Commission on Volun-

teer Service's promotion, advocacy and recognition committee makes selection recommendations, which go to the governor's office for final approval.

❑ *Promote, promote, promote!* Seek nominees via press releases, newsletters and e-mail messages. Have staff and committee members share information in their own networks. Promote the program on your website and all ways possible to ensure quality nominations are received.

34 Thank Donors With Inexpensive Gifts

A retired grandmother sends your organization $10 a month like clockwork. A third-grader gives $5 he saved from his allowance because he believes in your cause.

The success of most charities depends on countless loyal supporters such as these whose gifts — large and small — mean a great deal to you.

Saying thanks in a meaningful way needn't cost much. Here are some tokens of appreciation that can promote your organization while being affordable (depending upon quantities ordered, less than $2 each) and useful:

✓ **Calendar magnets.** Placed on a refrigerator or file cabinet, a full-year calendar bearing your logo and contact information is handy, durable and lightweight for mailing. Available in quantity from many vendors in 4" x 5" formats, they fit in envelopes with thank-you notes and keep your organization top-of-mind year-round.

✓ **Sticky note pads.** Isn't everyone always looking for a scrap of paper for a note or phone number? Bought in office supply stores, full packs can be expensive and may be a small luxury for some. Make their lives just a little easier with this convenient token. Use the top note to jot a heartfelt thank-you.

✓ **Mini mint logo tin.** Most supporters won't think of this gift as a signal that they need a breath mint, but appreciate having a handy size to stick in a pocket or purse after their favorite sub sandwich or Italian dinner. They will think of you whenever they use it.

✓ **Key-chain tools.** A tape measure, flashlight, screwdriver or sewing kit can do wonders in an emergency, but people rarely have them away from home. Think of items you need in a pinch, because chances are your contributors may need them, too.

✓ **Colorful dog tags.** Especially popular with children and teens, military-style dog tags with chains make a fun gift, and allow donors to wear their support for your organization. Regularly change tag colors so they can build a collection to wear all at once.

35 Engage Donor's Family In Recognition Efforts

When an individual or couple makes a major gift, ask for permission to involve their adult children in recognizing the gift. Doing so will serve as an important first step in cultivating those heirs to one day make similar gifts or to add to an existing family gift.

You can involve a donor's family by:

1. Inviting input on ways their parents might be recognized. Share some recognition options on which they can comment.

2. Making sure the entire family gets VIP treatment during any recognition events or ceremonies that take place: seating, public introductions and more.

3. Including the children in ongoing stewardship efforts: periodic reports on the impact of their parent's gift, invitations to your organization's events and so forth.

36 Simple Gesture May Reap Rewards In the Future

When thinking of ways to connect with donors and prospects, look beyond what will give your organization the greatest monetary return to consider gestures that will leave a lasting impression in donors' minds whenever they hear your organization's name.

In 2001, Vicki McNamara, executive director, Warren County United Way (Monmouth, IL), left a conference with the idea of giving without the expectation of getting something in return.

"I came up with an idea to go beyond our conventional cultivation techniques and began clipping newspaper articles, sending sympathy cards and congratulations to not only our donors but to prospective donors," says McNamara.

She reviews local newspapers for birthdays, anniversaries, youth or young adult sport or academic accomplishments and obituaries. She clips out such articles and sends them to the person featured (or his/her family) subject along with a personal note.

McNamara says the benefits of this gesture are immeasurable.

"The thanks we get back from the community are very gratifying," she says. "Not only have the donors been grateful but this experience has been gratifying emotionally and spiritually for me as well."

Source: Vicki McNamara, Executive Director, Warren County United Way, Monmouth, IL. Phone (309) 734-6364. E-mail: wcunitedway@juno.com

37 Offer Specialty Awards to Exceptional Members

Always be on the lookout for ways to recognize and share member accomplishments.

Staff with the Fox Cities Chamber of Commerce (Appleton, WI) grant specialty awards to members who contribute to the community, says Pamela Hull, vice president-membership & operations.

One such honor is the Athena Award, given annually to an exceptional businesswoman who: 1) has achieved the highest degree of professional excellence; 2) has assisted women in reaching their potential; and 3) possesses an impactful body of work.

"The Athena Award honors women business leaders for their exceptional contributions to their company, their industry, their community, to their chamber and to the advancement of women in business," Hull says. She adds that the chamber is among the charter group of chambers to host the awards since the program's inception in 1985.

More information about the Athena Award is available at www.athenafoundation.org.

Source: Pamela Hull, Vice President-Membership & Operations Manager, Fox Cities Chamber of Commerce, Appleton, WI. E-mail: phull@foxcitieschamber.com

38 Website Showcases Volunteers of the Month

Almost every volunteer-driven organization has some sort of recognition program. So what sets yours apart from others?

For the Humane Society of Williamson County (Leander, TX), volunteers are thanked for their contributions on a truly worldwide scale — through the humane society's website.

What originated as a volunteer-of-the-quarter program became a monthly recognition when Memi Cardenas signed on as volunteer coordinator for the humane society.

"My decision to change the program was based on the fact that we have so many volunteers who do such great jobs that I would much rather recognize 12 than four," says Cardenas. "I think the more I can recognize and give back to them, the more we will create a stronger team."

Each month, Cardenas looks back over the previous month, gathering feedback from staff on who has excelled, made a difference or who has been volunteering for a long time but hasn't been acknowledged.

"The volunteer of the month can be someone who takes on a lot of responsibility as a team leader or someone who does something as simple, but appreciated, as walking the dogs a few times a week," says Cardenas.

The online profiles feature a photo and a biography highlighting the volunteer, what he/she has done for the organization and how long he/she has been volunteering.

Cardenas says the program is a great morale booster for her volunteers. "I have volunteers come up and ask me how they can become the volunteer of the month. It is a great motivator to get the other volunteers to try and achieve that acknowledgement."

"Content not available in this edition"

Source: Memi Cardenas, Volunteer Coordinator, Humane Society of Williamson County, Leander, TX. Phone (512) 260-3602, ext. 106. E-mail: mcardenas@hswc.net

Volunteer of the Month features on the Humane Society of Williamson County website include photos, biographies and reasons why volunteers are being honored.

39 Make Your Dedication a Memorable Experience

It takes special acts of generosity to successfully complete a capital campaign. And those responsible for your campaign's success deserve special recognition. That's why a dedication ceremony should be well planned.

Whether you limit invitations or hope the entire community shows up, attention to detail is key. Consider these ideas as you plan your dedication event:

- Don't wait too long. Interest in a dedication will wane if people have already seen and experienced the completed project.

- Showcase those who made the most significant gifts by providing special name tags, reserved seating, escort service, public recognition and more.

- Add buzz by announcing the event will include an unveiling (e.g., revealing the name of the facility, a work of art or donor wall), or that you will be announcing the name of a generous — and to date, anonymous — donor.

- Offer tours, demonstrations and/or hands-on experiences to show off the completed project's full capabilities.

- Bring distinction to the event by asking those in leadership positions (e.g., mayor, governor, etc.) to attend and take part in the program.

- If the event is free and open to the public, make your citizenry aware of that in multiple ways — news releases, direct mail, ads, flyers, etc.

- Videotape the ceremony to send (or deliver) copies to major donors unable to attend.

- To commemorate the historic event, give attendees a limited-edition memento (e.g., work of art, framed photograph or paperweight).

40 Celebrate Anniversary of Building Dedication

The opening of your new or renovated facility shouldn't close the doors on recognitions.

A 20th anniversary celebration of the Fletcher Library on Arizona State University's West Campus (Phoenix, AZ) in March 2008 recognized the contributions of the Robert L. Fletcher family and the university's 20 years of service to the growing region, says Steve Des Georges, director of public relations and marketing.

Opened in 1988, the Fletcher Library is named in honor of the Fletcher family in recognition of their gift of land to the ASU Foundation. Proceeds of the sale established an endowment that provides funding in perpetuity to the library.

"The (anniversary) event brought a lot of attention to the library and how long it has been a part of the greater Phoenix metropolitan area," says Des Georges. "Any time you can bring a group of people together to celebrate an accomplishment or a milestone, you build a greater sense of pride for who you are and what you do. It was also a great way to reconnect with the Fletchers and others prominent in the library's founding."

Leading up to the event, three six-foot banners showcasing various stages of library construction were displayed in the library atrium along with posters of staff memories. Photo displays included pictures of library and staff, library construction, dedication ceremony and 10th anniversary celebration. Video displays showed College of Teacher Education and Leadership students interviewing the library's Director Marilyn Myers.

On celebration day, staff gathered for potluck lunch and to view displays of the library through the years, photos of 10th and 20th anniversary staffs, and to share predictions of what the library would be like in 2018. A short program at 4 p.m. included remarks by ASU Vice President Elizabeth Langland, Director Meyers, Associate Librarian Leslee Shell, family representative Bob Fletcher and Gerald McSheffery, the first vice president and architect of the library, followed by cake and refreshments.

"The event was staged in the late afternoon to allow more people to participate, but it was also an informal event that encouraged attendees to visit with others who have played a role in the growth of Fletcher Library and the West campus," says Des Georges.

Invitees included staff of all ASU libraries; staff, faculty and students of the ASU West campus; and the Dean's Advisory Board. About 100 people attended, including the library's entire staff, deans of the colleges and all the campus library directors.

The eight-member anniversary committee included the library director, associate librarians, library administrators, a library specialist, library marketing representative and the events manager for the West campus.

Sources: Stephen Des Georges, Director of Public Relations and Marketing, Arizona State University at the West Campus, Phoenix, AZ. Phone (602) 543-5220. E-mail: Stephen.Desgeorges@asu.edu
Janice Kasperski, Associate Librarian, Arizona State University, Phoenix, AZ. Phone (602) 543-8518.
E-mail: Janice.Kasperski@asu.edu

41 Annual Garden Celebration Features Volunteer Display

Look for ways to jazz up traditional volunteer events as a way to thank volunteers for their service and celebrate your volunteer-based organization.

To honor the volunteers who serve at St. Joseph's Health Centre Foundation (Guelph, Ontario, Canada), Volunteer Coordinator Carol McGuigan plans a luncheon.

The outdoor appreciation event relies on good weather and strong attendance of its 50 to 80 volunteers to make for a successful event held in the garden.

The theme "Volunteers … Caring, Sharing and Growing," is fitting for the garden celebration, McGuigan says.

As a special tribute, McGuigan creates a display that greets volunteers upon their arrival at the event. Located at the entrance of the garden, McGuigan fills the board with photos of volunteers in action throughout the year and adds inspirational quotes that will move the guests.

Follow these guidelines to prepare a display at your next volunteer appreciation event — the volunteers will feel special for the time and effort you put into it:

- Prepare a three-panel, table-top display board approximately 6-x-4 feet, allowing ample room to display your message.

- Use brightly colored graphics, fonts and borders with a garden theme, or a theme that matches your event, to give a cheerful and fun appearance.

- Keep in mind this special group's importance as the display is being prepared, creating a message of appreciation. This luncheon is devoted to your hardworking volunteers for their efforts!

Source: Carol McGuigan, Volunteer Coordinator, St. Joseph's Health Centre Foundation, Guelph, Ontario, Canada. Phone (519) 767-3424. E-mail: cmcguiga@sjhcg.ca. Website: www.sjhcg.ca

---

42 Host an Annual Event to Thank Endowment Donors

Just as you might host an annual event to thank all contributors at the $1,000-and-above level, consider hosting a similar event geared to the past year's endowment donors (assuming you have sufficient numbers to merit such an event). An endowment dinner or reception draws attention to the importance of building your endowment and also serves to recognize these important contributors.

You can use your event to:

- Point out endowment performance for the past year.

- Provide attendees with a printed handout that describes all named endowment funds and who supported each for the past year.

- Announce newly established endowment funds.

- Showcase the impact particular funds have on your nonprofit organization and the lives of those you serve.

- Generate publicity about your endowment by selectively inviting key media officials.

- Make special note of realized planned gifts for that year which have been earmarked for endowment purposes.

---

43 11 Ideas for Ground Breaking Ceremony Gifts

If you are planning a ground breaking ceremony following is a list of gift ideas for your event's attendees.

1. Construction-shaped stress balls imprinted with organization logo (available in hard hats, bricks, tool boxes, construction cones, etc.).

2. Plaques with metal hard hats, shovels or hammers attached.

3. Lucite paper weights etched with organization logo with embedded hard hats, shovels, etc.

4. Stonecast hard hat magnets, business card holders, etc.

5. Building replicas cast in stone.

6. Custom gold, pewter or silver shovels with a presentation box.

7. Shovel lapel pins.

8. Prints of the watercolor rendering of the new building.

9. Logo-imprinted hard hats.

10. A ceremonial shovel attached to a ribbon with organization logo, the words Ground Breaking Ceremony and date of the ceremony.

11. Miniature shovel and hard hat keychains imprinted with organization logo and date of the ceremony.

Offer Sweet Rewards

At Glencroft Retirement Community (Glendale, AZ), volunteers bank an impressive 50,000-plus hours each year. To show appreciation, Barb Lenards, director of community services, and her staff offer Tea Tuesdays and Thirsty Thursdays.

"Many of our volunteers live on campus," Lenards said. "This program is fun, offers volunteers a social opportunity and keeps older volunteers well hydrated."

Tuesday and Thursday afternoons, nearly 100 people gather in anticipation of the royal treatment.

"Our volunteer coordinator, Jeanne McMenimen, and I look forward to the volunteers stopping by," Lenards says. "It's an added way for us to be in contact with them and share some time together."

Lenards shares two favorite recipes sure to please your volunteers as well:

Grape Juice Crush
- 1 – 24 ounce white grape juice
- 1 cup orange juice
- ¼ cup lemon juice
- ½ cup sugar
- 1 quart ginger ale

Mix and stir juices until sugar is dissolved. Just before serving, add ginger ale. Serve over crushed ice. Serves 8.

Frozen Slush Tea
- 2 cups white sugar
- 7 cups water
- 4 tea bags
- 2 cups boiling water
- 1 (12 fluid ounce) can frozen lemonade concentrate
- 1 (12 fluid ounce) can frozen orange juice concentrate

Put seven cups water in large saucepan, and heat on high until boiling. Add sugar and stir until dissolved; set aside to cool. Place tea bags in two cups boiling water, and let steep until at desired strength.

In a large bowl, mix together sugar water, tea, lemonade and orange juice concentrates. Place in freezer container and freeze overnight. To serve, place several scoops into a tall glass and fill with any clear carbonated beverage. Serves 16.

Source: Barb Lenards, Director of Community Services at Glencroft Retirement Community, Glendale, AZ. Phone (623) 847-3004. E-mail: barb@glencroft.com

 ## Hold Raffle to Fund Volunteer Recognition

Look for creative, crowd-pleasing ways to generate attention and funds for your volunteer program.

At the Steppingstone Museum (Havre de Grace, MD), for example, an annual raffle helps raise money for recognition programs for its 100 regular volunteers who serve the 300 members of the museum.

The recognition programs help keep volunteers motivated and serve as a way to thank them for their service, says Linda Noll, executive director. Volunteers are recognized each quarter with gifts of T-shirts, hats or other small tokens based on the number of hours they've served within that time frame. At the museum's annual dinner and volunteer awards ceremony, volunteers receive awards for hours served that year.

"Museum programs such as school tours and other educational programs, not to mention all special events, would not be possible without our volunteers," Noll says.

The museum holds an annual raffle to cover the expense of their volunteer recognition program. Museum artisans donate a handcrafted item for the raffle so there are at least six raffle prizes available. Raffle tickets are sold to the membership and to the public where approximately 800 tickets are sold at $1 each, raising a total of $800 each year.

Noll recommends tips to host a successful volunteer recognition raffle:

1. Offer raffle items that are truly unique or handcrafted, making them a one-of-a-kind, desirable item to participants.

2. Keep the ticket price no higher than $10 per chance. Keeping the ticket price low allows for easier ticket sales and offers the buyer more opportunities to win.

3. Make the buyer aware that all proceeds fund the volunteer recognition program.

More Creative Recognition Ideas

In addition to recognizing volunteers through special events and awards, Linda Noll, executive director at Steppingstone Museum (Havre de Grace, MD), shares other ways she and her colleagues recognize volunteers:

- Giving volunteers a sense of ownership in the museum. If volunteers feel they are an instrumental part of the organization, they will tell their friends and family about the museum and possibly recruit them as volunteers as well.
- Ask volunteers to serve on the board and on committees.
- Enlist volunteer suggestions and assistance to help with special events and tours at your organization.

Source: Linda Noll, Executive Director, Steppingstone Museum, Havre de Grace, MD. Phone (410) 939-2299. E-mail: steppingstonemuseum@msn.com

---

46 Recognition Event Considerations

Have you been debating whether or not to allow volunteers to bring guests to your annual recognition event? Consider these differing viewpoints:

- A volunteer-only event gives volunteers a chance to focus on each other and get to know one another.

- By allowing volunteers to bring a guest, you can use the event as a recruitment tool. The event is a perfect way for potential volunteers to see the benefits of becoming a volunteer with your organization.

47 Recognition Tip

- Mark "Advance Copy" or "Confidential" on communications you send to key members. Your board members, chapter leaders, and others in leadership positions, as well as members who donate at higher levels will appreciate this top-level treatment. These messages will say to them, "You are important to us," and add value to their memberships. Take it a step further and add a personal note (e.g., "James, I'd love to hear your opinion on this ad. Give me a call by Aug. 1 at 555-1212! ~ Susan").

---

48 Engage Major Donors With Capital Project Scrapbook

Looking for a way to steward your capital project donors? Laurie Rogers, director of development, Peter Paul Development Center (Richmond, VA), suggests starting a scrapbook of your building's progress.

Rogers has created a photo scrapbook for the last three capital projects she has been involved with in Richmond. At the ground breaking, she presents donors with a three-ring binder. She then mails photo updates to them — already three-hole punched — at least once a month.

"I include a note about how things are going," says Rogers. "In this economy, any progress is good progress." Donors unable to attend the ground breaking receive the binder by mail or a personal delivery.

Rogers suggests scheduling hardhat tours once a quarter for donors to see the progress for themselves: "Even if they don't come to campus, they know that you are tending this investment that they have so graciously and generously made in your project," she says. "In all three capital projects I've been involved in, the message has always been the same — gratitude. The donors have been quite appreciative of this effort."

Source: Laurie Rogers, Director of Development, Peter Paul Development Center, Richmond, VA. Phone (804) 780-1195. E-mail: plrogers@earthlink.net

---

49 Choose Appropriate Gifts for First-time Prospect Visits

Q. What do you suggest as a small gift for a first-time prospect/donor visit?

"Whatever gift you choose to bring along on a first visit with a prospect or donor needs to have a reason and tie-in with your mission. The more creative and personalized the gift, the better.... The key is to make the gift useful and something they will touch often and will catch other people's eyes and elicit inquiry.

"One of my clients, the Phi Beta Kappa Society, gave out letter openers, leather bookmarks, paperweights, a history of the society book and a collection of addresses by famous members, for example.

Because The American Scholar and The Key Reporter magazines published book reviews, we had hundreds of beautiful books that needed to be disposed of, so I took ones that I knew would be of interest to the donor prospect with whom I was meeting and had it inscribed by the secretary of the society. Those went over very well.

"When I was working with Washington National Cathedral, I brought a Christmas ornament that featured the cathedral. Every time they would unpack it during gift-giving time, they would recall my visit and gift. Similarly, when I served on the Episcopal Diocesan Stewardship Commission, we had leatherette checkbook covers with Diocesan and Episcopal shields and a scripture verse that dealt with tithing printed in gold on the cover so that every time they pulled out their checkbook, they were reminded of giving to the church and the good work their tithe was doing.

"When I was at American University, I asked the bookstore for five extra books written by a faculty member. I had them generically autographed with a message, 'Best wishes and many thanks for your support of scholarship at American University!' and I would hand those out at donor visits."

— Jared B. Hughes, Principal, Bellwether Fundraising (Takoma Park, MD)

---

50   Share Awards, Recognition With Current, Potential Members

When your organization receives an award or is recognized in a unique way, make sure to spread the word. Publicizing these accolades will remind members and would-be members how hard you are working on their behalf and also give members a sense of pride in your organization.

In late 2008, officials with Lee's Summit Chamber of Commerce (Lee's Summit, MO) learned the organization had been named 2008 Missouri Chamber of the Year. "As soon as we learned we were the winner, we announced it at the monthly membership luncheon," says Leann Northway, director of communications.

Immediately after the luncheon announcement, chamber staff went to work sharing the news with members in a variety of methods, including:

- Mentioning the award on the front cover of the chamber's newsletter;

- Sending press releases mentioning the honor to local media;

- Featuring the news on electronic billboards, which are located on heavily traveled highways, for two weeks;

- Adding mention of the award in staff e-mail signatures and at the bottom of all press releases sent out during the following months.

Chamber staff spread the word about the honor without incurring any costs for their efforts. Use of the electronic billboard announcements was made available at no cost by their owners, while the rest of the publicity efforts were created in-house.

Publicizing such news is vital to member-driven organizations, says Northway.

"It is very important that all our members know we are working diligently for the success of their business and that this honor recognizes those efforts," she says, adding that anecdotal feedback from members regarding the award has been positive.

Along with the advertising methods mentioned above, Northway recommends asking long-term members for their ideas and support in publicizing your awards.

"Use all mediums possible," she says. "Every chance you get to mention it — in meetings, on agendas, public speaking engagements, e-blasts — do it. Today people get their news from a variety of sources. It is so important to make sure you hit all those sources."

Source: Leann Northway, Director of Communications, Lee's Summit Chamber of Commerce, Lee's Summit, MO. Phone (816) 524-2424. E-mail: LNorthway@lschamber.com

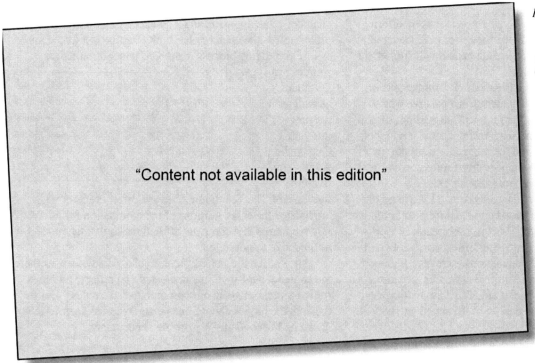

"Content not available in this edition"

Featuring an article in the monthly newsletter is one of many ways staff with Lee's Summit Chamber of Commerce (Lee's Summit, MO) spread the word to members and others that the chamber received honors as 2008 Missouri Chamber of the Year.

51 10 Ways to Show You Care

1. Write a thank-you note to a volunteer's spouse and/or children saying how much you appreciate the time their loved one has given you.

2. Invite volunteers of all ages to your recognition event and hold it when (nearly) everyone can come.

3. Put together a DVD of staff and clients saying thanks" to volunteers. Premiere it at your recognition event and play it in your volunteer break room.

4. Track the dollar value of your volunteers' service and present them with a fake check at your annual recognition event.

5. As much as your schedule allows, check in on them as they are volunteering to offer words of thanks, a fresh cup of coffee or other type of pat on the back.

6. Have volunteers invite a friend to the annual recognition event. This is also a recruiting tool as guests see how great your program is.

7. Recognize off-hour volunteers (persons who fill in evenings and weekends) with unexpected perks such as treats in the break room or a visit and hand shake from your CEO.

8. Thank your computer-savvy volunteers with a quick e-mail.

9. Every time one of your volunteers makes your organization's internal newsletter, print a copy of the article for your volunteer.

10. If appropriate for your organization, say thanks in a silly way! Ideas:

   ✓ Slap smiley-face stickers on volunteers' lapels or grab a colorful bouquet of flowers at the supermarket to add boutonnieres to volunteer uniforms to brighten everyone's day.

   ✓ Fill a cooler with ice cream bars and deliver to on-duty volunteers (be sure to include sugar- and fat-free choices).

   ✓ Hand out helium balloons with a handwritten note of thanks and a small bag of candy attached.

52 Offer Members a Way to Recognize Key Staff

Allow your members a way to honor their staff by offering an award that lets them extol the virtues of their key employees or co-workers. This added-value benefit will strengthen your membership package.

The Northern Kentucky Chamber of Commerce (Fort Mitchell, KY) offers its 1,900 members a positive way to honor their key personnel. Through its Outstanding Administrative Professional of the Year Award, chamber members nominate administrative staff for recognition. All nominees are treated at the annual Administrative Professionals Breakfast held on Administrative Professionals Day.

The 2010 event, taking place on April 21, "will be our fourth year giving out the award and the third year holding the event," says Tara Sorrell Proctor, coordinator of workforce, education & health care solutions at the chamber. "We typically receive 40 to 50 nominations each year. Members love nominating their administrative assistants, because it's a way of recognizing their hard work. The administrative professionals, even those who don't win the award, are honored just to be nominated."

The winner, honored at the annual breakfast event, receives a plaque and prizes valued at more than $200.

The chamber advertises the event on the home page of its website, at chamber meetings and events, through chamber-related e-mails and a contact list of administrative professionals the chamber has built over the last five years.

"Our judging process involves a panel of human resources professionals, as well as the previous year's Outstanding Administrative Professional of The Year winner," says Sorrell Proctor. "They are handed the essay portions of the nomination forms. We remove names and company affiliations so that the process is as objective as possible.

To view the online nomination form for the administrative professional of the year award presented by the Northern Kentucky Chamber of Commerce (Fort Mitchell, KY), go to www.nkychamber.com and click on the link, Nominate Your Administrative Professional.

"It is still extremely difficult to choose a winner, as there are so many hard-working, dedicated and reliable administrative professionals in our community," she notes. "But in the end, the judges choose one person who has seemed to go above and beyond any reasonable expectations."

Source: Tara Sorrell Proctor, Coordinator, Workforce, Education & Health Care Solutions, Northern Kentucky Chamber of Commerce, Fort Mitchell, KY. Phone (859)578-6399.
E-mail: tsorrell@nkychamber.com. Website: www.nkychamber.com

53 Focus on Donors Individually When Recognizing Major Gifts

Q. We are holding an event at which we will be recognizing two donors, one who gave $1 million, and one who gave $100,000. How do we recognize both donors appropriately at the same event?

"Hold separate recognition ceremonies that feature each donor. You wouldn't want to have the ceremonies at the same time because it would mean both donors would be sharing the spotlight, which wouldn't be in the best interest of the donor who gave the larger amount. If you have to hold the ceremonies at the same time, you might want to host a private luncheon or dinner with the president and the $1 million donor and his or her family either before or following the event. This elevates the larger donor's generosity to a higher level. The lower-level donor could be invited to a luncheon or dinner with the dean of the school benefiting from the gift."

— Leanne Poon, Manager, Donor Relations & Stewardship, University of British Columbia (Vancouver, BC)

"Dollar level alone cannot decide the course of action. At either of those donation levels, you should have some idea of the relationship of gift size to potential as well as what's most meaningful to and in keeping with the personality of the donor.

"The $100,000 gift might have been an extreme stretch for that donor, the most they can ever give. The $1 million gift might have been a moderate or even typical gift for the other donor. Each donor knows which category he or she is in. If the smaller gift was a stretch gift and the larger donor gets more recognition, what message does that convey about the values of your organization?

"There are more folks out there who might be able to consider a $100,000 gift — even as a stretch gift — under certain circumstances than a $1 million gift. Don't make the prize too out of reach for them."

— Mary Kay Filter Dietrich, Vice President for Development & External Relations, Urban League of Greater Pittsburgh (Pittsburgh, PA)

54 Five Effective Volunteer Appreciation Ideas

Without a doubt, volunteers are an invaluable resource to your nonprofit organization.
Try these simple ways to show your valued volunteers exactly how much they mean to your organization:

✓ Frame a photo of the volunteer in action serving clients or helping your organization, along with a handwritten thank-you note mounted within the frame.

✓ Gather all volunteers and staff to join in an impromptu round of applause for a job well done directed toward a specific volunteer or group of volunteers who have recently completed or are in the middle of a major project or difficult task.

✓ Create a giant banner of thanks to include the names of all volunteers and handwritten greetings from staff, clients and visitors.

✓ Ask a school class to adopt your nonprofit and create a poster about the service of volunteers to post for your volunteers to enjoy.

✓ Ask a community leader to take a special volunteer to lunch in appreciation of his or her selfless efforts for your cause.

55 Offer a Sabbatical To Deserving Volunteers

Colleges and universities, even some companies, have offered sabbaticals — an extended period of leave from one's customary work — to deserving faculty and employees for years. They're offered as a "rest" or an opportunity to acquire new skills.

Why not use the sabbatical concept for volunteers who have served your organization for a long period, as a way to give them a deserved break?

Here's one scenario of how a volunteer sabbatical might work.

1. To give your sabbatical the importance it deserves, limit them (e.g., one sabbatical per year or one sabbatical every six months).

2. Assign the selection of your sabbatical recipient to a committee who can review a list of deserving nominees.

3. Announce the sabbatical recipient(s) at your annual volunteer recognition event.

4. Get one or more businesses to sponsor your sabbatical program by underwriting any costs associated with it. Some of those costs might include:

    • A cash honorarium and/or gift for the sabbatical recipient.
    • The cost of the actual award to be given to the recipient.
    • The cost associated with some educational opportunity for the recipient.
    • Possible travel expenses.

56 Volunteer Spotlight Lets Staff Recognize Volunteers

With 700 volunteers, knowing each one on a personal level — and sharing that knowledge with others — can be a challenge. One way to do so is to ask the staff members who work with the volunteers to help.

Every four to six weeks, Mandi Lindner, community relations coordinator, United Community Center (UCC) of Milwaukee, WI, showcases a different volunteer for the organization's Volunteer Spotlight.

Winners are featured in a newsletter article, in a biography posted on UCC's website and on the electronic billboard that runs in the community center lobby.

Program coordinators are encouraged to nominate their volunteers for the honor. Once a volunteer is nominated, he/she fills out an informational Volunteer Spotlight form. The form asks personal information, plus questions about their volunteer experience, including:

✓ How many years have you volunteered with UCC?

✓ Describe what you do on a typical volunteering shift.

✓ What do you enjoy most about volunteering at UCC?

✓ What keeps you coming back?

✓ Why would you encourage others to volunteer with UCC?

✓ Do you have a favorite story or client you'd like to tell others about?

Lindner uses the information for the newsletter article and biography. She changes the form depending on the answers. If a volunteer writes detailed responses, she sometimes will make the article a question-and-answer piece. Other times she'll incorporate information about the program involving the volunteer.

Through the Volunteer Spotlight recognition, Lindner says her organization is able to get some personal information about the agency volunteers, recognize them and get staff involved in seeing how great a job the volunteers are doing.

Source: Mandi Lindner, Community Relations Coordinator, United Community Center, Milwaukee, WI. Phone (414) 384-3100. E-mail: mlindner@unitedcc.org

57 Don't Wait to Recognize Volunteers

Don't miss an opportunity to recognize your volunteers. As soon as they do something special, let them know.

Besides providing a yearly volunteer recognition event, Lynn Preminger, volunteer coordinator, Jewish Family Services (Hartford, CT), sends special notes and cards to volunteers whenever she sees or learns that they have gone beyond the call of duty.

Preminger says she likes to give volunteers recognition when it's unexpected. She realizes that some volunteers don't want to be recognized publicly and tries to let them know personally when she's proud of their work.

When Preminger calls a volunteer to thank or recognize him/her, she also shares the achievement with a spouse or child who may answer the phone as well.

Source: Lynn Preminger, Volunteer Coordinator, Jewish Family Services, West Hartford, CT. Phone (860) 236-1920, ext. 37. E-mail: lpreminger@jfshartford.org

58 Appoint a Kudos Manager

If you work with large numbers of volunteers, you might want someone, perhaps a hand-picked volunteer, to manage your kudos procedures.

It becomes the responsibility of your kudos manager to see that appropriate thanks and recognition are given to all volunteers. It doesn't mean, however, that your kudos manager is always the one doing the thanking. That individual simply oversees the process and notifies appropriate individuals to say thanks and recognize deserving volunteers in appropriate ways.

The kudos manager can select from a varied menu of thank-you and recognition ideas depending on why an individual is being recognized. Those forms of recognition may include but not be limited to:

- A face-to-face thank you from your CEO or a board member.
- Nomination for a special award.
- Personal notes from someone selected by the kudos manager.
- Letters of praise to a volunteer's employer.
- A signed certificate of appreciation.
- Gifts.
- A special volunteer perk: designated parking space, office space, business cards, etc.

59 Say Thanks With Many Voices

Writing notes of thanks is one of the best ways to tell donors how valuable they are to your organization. But the activity can also establish a valuable connection for your volunteers and those you serve. Involve everyone in the act. Have volunteers write notes of thanks. Invite those you serve to come in and write a note or two when they have time. You'll find few other activities that so strongly reinforce your connections to these constituents.

While formal recognition of major gifts is crucial, small personal gestures, such as handwritten notes from volunteers, can make a big impact on major donors.

Dear Mr. and Mrs. Franco,

I'm a volunteer at the Lansing Humane Society, and want to let you know how much your gift to our building campaign means to me and the hundreds of animals I help take care of each year.

When our new building is completed this summer, we'll have outdoor exercise areas for our dogs and cats to socialize and exercise — something we only dream of offering them now.

And we'll have four private "romping rooms" where people can interact one-on-one with animals to see if they're a good match. I have no doubt this will increase our adoption numbers and give many more strays a good home.

I'd love to meet you in person. Drop by any Saturday, 8-11 a.m., and ask for me by name!

Thanks again!

Sandra Berginski

60 Recognize the Efforts of Long-distance Volunteers

Although recognizing the efforts of volunteers assisting you from far-off locations is an important component of volunteer management, doing so can be challenging.

Create a menu of recognition strategies for these more distant volunteers. Examples may include:

✓ A lapel pin or piece of jewelry that designates their relationship to your agency.

✓ Scheduled phone calls (to discuss business) and unscheduled calls (to pat them on the back).

✓ Posting information on your website that recognizes their valuable contributions.

✓ Insider news sent regularly to let them know they're special.

✓ Phone calls from higher ups (board members, the CEO, and others) thanking them.

✓ Publishing their names as "VIVs" (very important volunteers).

✓ Placing ads in their local newspapers that publicly thank them.

✓ Sending an occasional photo of something special taking place at your facility.

✓ Mass-producing a video of a special event or ceremony and sending copies.

✓ Sending a card and personal note during unexpected times.

61 Say Thanks With a Book Plate

Celebrate your donors' birthdays and anniversaries or send condolences by purchasing a book plate inscribed with the donor's name to be placed in a book in your organization's library.

Research donors' interests to find books that best fit them. Send donors a letter telling about the book plate. Enclose a small mesh gift bag holding a 4-by-6-inch frame containing a certificate you can create on your computer listing the name of the donor, the occasion, the date, and the name of the book.

62 Nothing Seems to Beat a Handwritten Note

People are smart. They have seen enough "personalized" form letters — with their names inserted into the body of the letter — to know that they are one of many, maybe thousands, receiving the same letter. That's why you can't beat a handwritten letter when you really want to make your message personal.

Think about the handwritten correspondence you've received. Pretty impressive, isn't it? And this personal touch is even more impressive today, in a world of e-mail, computer-generated correspondence and other forms of communication.

63 Recognition Gallery of Honor Showcases Donors

Consider creating a recognition wall to permanently honor your major donors.

Since 2004, persons who give $5,000 or more to Carroll Hospital Center (Westminster, MD) have had their names placed on its Gallery of Honor, a 20-foot wide, five-foot tall recognition wall located in the most visible spot in the hospital — the outer lobby.

Sherri Hosfeld Joseph, director of development, says they created the display to encourage donors' giving and inspire them to give more, reaching to achieve a higher level on the display. Cumulative giving amounts are based on gifts made since 1989, which she says is as far back as the foundation's electronic records go.

"We make sure our consistent donors are aware of the wall, and let new donors know that a gift at a certain level will get them on the wall," she says. "We also place brochures in a rack by the wall so that visitors can grab one if they are interested in knowing how to make a gift."

The honor wall recognizes eight giving levels:

1. Chairman's Circle, $1 million or more
2. Sinnott Fellows, $500,000 to $999,999
3. President's Club, $250,000 to $499,999
4. 1961 Society, $100,000 to $249,999
5. Stewards Club, $50,000 to $99,999
6. Galen Club, $25,000 to $49,999
7. Sponsor, $10,000 to $24,999
8. Patron, $5,000 to $9,999

When donors make gifts that move them up a giving level, Hosfeld Joseph says, development staff place new name plaques in the appropriate giving spots, then send the old plaques to the donors as a gift, along with an invitation to come see the gallery. Donors who include the hospital in estate plans are honored on the wall under a Bridge Builders listing.

Development staff add names to the wall twice a year by running a cumulative giving report of $5,000-plus, says Hosfeld Joseph. The magnetic plaques, engraved with donors' names, cost $25 to $80, depending on the size.

Source: Sherri Hosfeld Joseph, Director of Development, Carroll Hospital Center & Carroll Hospice, Westminster, MD. Phone (410) 871-6200. E-mail: Sjoseph@carrollhospitalcenter.org

---

Gallery of Honor Stats

What: Gallery of Recognition Donor Wall for Carroll Hospital Center (Westminster, MD)

Why: To recognize cumulative gifts of $5,000-plus

Purchased from: Honorcraft (www.honorcraft.com)

Dimensions: 20 feet wide, 5 feet tall

Cost of each name plaque: $25 to $80 based on size

Cost of system: $40,000

Levels of giving: Eight ($5,000 to $1 million-plus); plus estate gifts

---

"Content not available in this edition"

---

64   Share Photos That Celebrate Campaign-funded Renovation

For the first-ever capital campaign for Bryant University (Smithfield, RI), staff commissioned a photographer to take photos of the changing campus landscape over the four years of the campaign and create a portfolio of seasonal campus photos.

At the campaign conclusion, a framed, matted set of four photos of the university's renovated campus, representing the four seasons, was given to all donors of $25,000 and above, as well as trustees, campaign volunteers and other high-profile donors, says Jennifer M. Fusco, associate director of stewardship.

The photos were either presented at the campaign finale gala, or, if the person did not attend the gala, hand-delivered by the assigned gift officer (if applicable). If delivery could not be arranged in that three-month time frame, recipients received the photos by mail with a letter signed by the university president.

Fusco says they continue to use the collection of photos in various publications, such as the alumni magazine, a campaign recap piece and a campus calendar.

Source: Jennifer M. Fusco, Associate Director of Stewardship, Bryant University, Smithfield, RI. Phone (401) 232-6812. E-mail: jfusco@bryant.edu

65   Elm Tree Society Thanks, Stewards Donors

Honor rolls, luncheons and gifts are just a few of the ways to thank and steward donors.

Staff with Scripps College (Claremont, CA) created a donor recognition society that uses those three methods and more. Currently some 300 members strong, the Elm Tree Society began in the early 1990s to honor and highlight planned giving donors and as a way for the college to show its appreciation to donors through elite events and gifts.

Allyson Simpson, director of planned giving, shares the details of the society:

What are the criteria to belong to the Elm Tree Society?

"A person must have made a life-income gift (e.g., charitable gift annuity, charitable remainder trust, etc.) or have communicated a testamentary bequest intention, including the designation of the college as the beneficiary of a life insurance policy, commercial annuity or a retirement plan."

What does the college do with the society?

"We use the society to steward existing donors, thank and cultivate them for additional planned gifts. It has an aura of 'specialness' about it, especially with respect to the appreciation gifts we give members, which usually bear the special society logo."

What does the college do for members of the society?

"First, we feature the members prominently in the annual Honor Roll of Donors. Second, we hold at least two lunch/program events a year on campus and one or more lunch events in off-campus locations where we have a critical mass geographically of members. Usually the president of the college welcomes and thanks those in attendance at the on-campus events. Third, once a year... we present all members (in person or by mail if they cannot attend the lunch event) with a recognition gift that identifies them as society members."

Why is this society successful?

"We engage in constant, year-round stewardship and appreciation. Our members come to anticipate the events and the gifts, and seem to really enjoy both and feel good about what they have done for the future of the college."

What challenges do you face with this society? How are you overcoming them?

"Planning and executing the events and staying in touch with members who live out of the area. Because the membership is predominantly elderly, sometimes our attendance is lower than we'd like. It's difficult for some of our more elderly constituents to get to campus or the event site. We try to schedule lunch events in conjunction with other programs on campus so there will be other persons coming to campus who might be able to drive the more elderly members who do not drive anymore. We also try to match people up geographically so they can come together.... When we send gifts to out-of-area members who can't make it to campus, we always send a warm letter thanking them again for their thoughtful gift and reminding them how important they are to the future of the college."

What advice do you have for organizations interested in creating a similar society?

- "Select a name that means something to the constituent body, since planned giving is all about legacy, emotional attachment and ultimate gifts. Our name comes from the Elm Tree Lawn on campus where every commencement is held.
- "Publicize the society to existing planned giving donors and to likely planned giving prospects.
- "Steward, steward, steward on a consistent basis and show appreciation in important and visible, but relatively inexpensive, ways. We produce official membership certificates on a desktop computer that are signed by the college president. I try to choose recognition gifts that are useful for older persons and are inexpensive per unit, but still very classy, in the college's colors with the Elm Tree Society logo prominently displayed."

Source: Allyson Simpson, Director of Planned Giving, Scripps College, Claremont, CA. Phone (909) 621-8400. E-mail: allyson.simpson@scrippscollege.edu

66 Make Impact With End-of-campaign Thanks

Go beyond the expected to thank your major donors.

Staff with The College of William and Mary (Williamsburg, VA) took special steps to thank donors to the college's $500 million campaign that ended in June 2007, says Lesley Atkinson, director of donor relations, "An art professor here and her class created 10 prints of campus scenes which were numbered and put in a portfolio and sent to members of the college's National Campaign Committee along with a thank-you note from the college president for their service."

In addition, she says, they thanked their campaign donors and volunteers by:

- Inviting the 15-member campaign steering committee to a dinner where they were given unique hand-blown vases in the school's colors of green and gold.

- Giving the campaign chairman a professionally produced three-ring binder embossed with his name and the campaign logo containing a chronology of the campaign through photos, invitations and campaign newsletter.

- Hiring a nationally-known artist who lives in Williamsburg and is also an alumna to create three pottery pieces, hand painted with King William and Queen Mary, to give to their campaign donors. Donors of $500,000 and above were given large chargers. Donors of $250,000 were given medium chargers, and donors of $100,000 were given porringers.

"Most of these gifts were hand delivered by development officers along with a thank-you letter from our president," says Atkinson. "Donors loved them."

Source: Lesley Atkinson, Director of Donor Relations, The College of William and Mary, Williamsburg, VA. Phone (757) 221-7696. E-mail: ljatki@wm.edu

67 Say Thank You in Special Ways

While expressing appreciation to donors — even major donors — needn't be expensive, it should be sincere and special. Make donor recognition a personal and genuine experience. Here's a sampling of ways to say, "We're so grateful for your friendship:"

- Regional books, magazines or newspaper subscriptions for donors from your region who have since relocated to another part of the country/world.

- A packet of seeds accompanying a personal note: "Your gift sowed seeds that will benefit others for generations to come."

- A named tree planted in tribute or in memory of someone.

- A video or photo album of a project's construction or renovation, start to finish.

- Personalized gift baskets.

- A hand-selected card signed by board members, employees and clients.

- A personal message on a marquee or outdoor billboard.

- A limited-edition drawing of a local/regional landmark.

- Special recognition on your website.

68 Offer Temporary Stand-ins for Recognition Displays

Q. "Can you share some ideas for temporary donor recognition displays for a building dedication ceremony?"

"If the building has a space to connect a flat-screen TV, you could do a nice presentation loop that features donors and the areas to which they have given. After the ceremony, switch the display screen over to building announcements and smart-teaching technology."

— *Lydia Palmer, Director of Development Communications, Rochester Institute of Technology (Rochester, NY)*

"While I was director of publications at Tampa Preparatory School (Tampa, FL), our engraved donor plaques weren't available in time for our building dedication ceremony, so we created small foam-core signs that provided a general idea of what their actual plaque would look like. They were very well-received and a cost-effective way to display our named areas of the school. Donors didn't complain and were very happy with the temporary sign until the engraved ones were available."

— *Jaci DaCosta, Director of Communications, Ursuline Academy (Dedham, MA)*

69 Labels Draw Awareness to Volunteer Efforts

Consider labeling your volunteer-assembled items and volunteer-created projects to draw attention to volunteers' efforts within your organization.

Volunteers at LifeCare Medical Center (Roseau, MN) fulfill a great array of tasks. Whether assembling information folders, admission packets, pamphlets or filling plastic eggs for the annual Easter egg hunt, they place a sticker on the item that reads, "Assembled by the caring hands of our Volunteers at LifeCare Medical Center."

"These labels trigger the minds of those utilizing the information that a volunteer's hands created that item," says Pam Sando, volunteer coordinator, "drawing awareness to our volunteer efforts and also putting our name on each item."

> Assembled by the caring hands of our Volunteers at LifeCare Medical Center

Source: Pam Sando and Terry Lamppa, Volunteer Coordinators, LifeCare Medical Center, Roseau, MN. Phone (218) 463-4714. E-mail: Volunteer@lifecaremc.com

70 Engage Members With Chapter Recognition Program

The Association of Government Accountants (AGA) in Alexandria, VA, manages 100 chapters comprising more than 14,000 members who are dedicated to the mission of providing quality education, fostering professional development and certification and supporting standards as well as research to advance government accountability.

By offering each chapter specific goals to achieve in all areas of chapter management through its 20-year-old chapter recognition program, the AGA has strengthened its chapter base and retained its members.

Jessica Jones, chapter services manager, answers questions about the program:

What is AGA's chapter recognition program?

"It is a framework for chapters, which, if followed, can result in a well-rounded chapter program each year. This non-competitive program consists of eight areas: chapter leadership, education, certification, communications, membership, early careers, community service and awards. Credits for various activities in each category are entered quarterly into an online reporting system by a chapter representative. Chapters that meet and exceed goals are recognized at AGA's annual Professional Development Conference and Exposition."

What is the purpose of the chapter recognition program?

"We developed our program in order to help chapters offer their membership a strong program throughout the year. If a chapter is struggling in one area, they can always turn to the program for suggestions on what they should be doing. We've also found that it helps chapters stay active by promoting friendly competition on who can be the most active. For AGA, recruiting younger members is key since so many baby boomers are retiring. Last year, we separated our early career initiatives out from the membership portion of the program so chapters would place more emphasis on them. Since this is a new area for our chapters, we included goals such as job shadowing, developing a mentor program and participating in career fairs to offer suggestions on how to reach out to younger people in their community. Since the chapters want to obtain these credits, they are more willing to hold more of these activities and are attracting people who don't know about AGA."

What milestones must your chapters reach in order to fulfill the recognition program?

"The program comprises eight areas and chapters must have credits in all of those areas to qualify for an award. We also have various award levels (platinum, gold, silver, etc.) that chapters can obtain, depending on how many credits they acquire throughout the year."

Does the recognition program aid in recruitment or retention?

"In our membership category, chapters can obtain credits for holding recruitment and retention events. We also add credits for chapters which have reached certain recruitment and retention goals by the end of the year. The goals are based on the size of the chapter and what is reasonable for them. One of the goals in the membership portion is to reach out to chapter members who were suspended at the end of the membership year. In order to obtain credits in this section, chapter committee chairs make personal phone calls and send e-mail messages to members on the suspended list. Sometimes just a personal touch or reminder makes the members feel that they really are a part of the association and they renew their membership."

How does your chapter program benefit the individual chapter itself and its leaders?

"The program ensures that emphasis is placed on all aspects of an association including education, communications, chapter leadership, community service, etc. This way, there isn't too much weight placed on one program area. We ask that chapters use the program as a planning tool for the next year and to involve the officers-elect in order to help them know what they're getting into by taking a leadership role. Seeing what is being done in the current year helps them plan what they should be doing when their term starts."

Source: Jessica Jones, Chapter Services Manager, Alexandria, VA. Phone (703) 684-6931. E-mail: jjones@agacgfm.org

Discover Heartfelt Methods to Recognize Your Volunteers

 What heartfelt methods do you use to recognize your volunteers and let them know how much you appreciate them?

"Each year the Laramie County Library hosts a celebration to honor the library volunteers. To keep costs down, the staff at the library contributes the food and prizes at the celebration. We also have integrated community-based, library-sponsored and nationally recognized awards as part of their recognition.

"For instance, Laramie County Library became a certified organization for the Presidential Volunteer Service Award, a privilege that costs nothing but a bit of paperwork and persistence.... Each volunteer who donates a certain amount of time gets a certificate signed by the president of the United States as well as a bronze, silver or gold pin. The volunteers are impressed and truly honored by this award. It gives them pride of accomplishment and a prestigious nationally recognized honor all at a minimal cost to the library.

"We also offer library-sponsored honors. Volunteers who work consistently for at least six months earn library staff privilege, which means they get to order discounted books, check out DVDs for free and never get charged overdue fines. It also means they are considered staff, which is even more valuable to some."

— *Julie Eatmon, Volunteer Specialist, Laramie County Library System (Cheyenne, WY)*

"Our teen volunteers create handmade birthday and anniversary (with our organization) cards to recognize our volunteers on a monthly basis. We recently acquired a small grant for our Teen Volunteer Program providing us the funds to purchase the craft items necessary for these and other projects.

"I also contact all local mortuaries in our area and ask them to provide the funds to have a catered meal for our volunteer appreciation dinner during Volunteer Appreciation Week in April. This has been done for several years now and they are happy to accommodate us. We have also had our staff serve the volunteers.

"We have had potlucks for the volunteers with the staff bringing the food. These are lots of fun."

— *Carolyn Kahla, Manager of Volunteers, Hospice of the Valleys (Murrieta, CA)*

 ## Unique Ways to Thank Your Campaign Steering Committee

At the end of your multi-year capital campaign, thank members of your campaign steering committee or other key players with a thoughtful gift such as:

A Personalized Symbolic Award: Therese O'Malley, director of benefactor relations, Northwestern Memorial Foundation (Chicago, IL), says at the end of a seven-year campaign that raised $206.4 million against a $150 million goal, they presented steering committee members with a custom-made crystal pyramid award engraved with the campaign total, a message of gratitude and the member's name. "Like many other fundraising shops, we used the campaign pyramid to track our fundraising success throughout the campaign," O'Malley says. "As this became a symbol of our progress, it seemed to be an appropriate item to honor our campaign steering committee members for their years of hard work."

Meaningful Framed Photographs: Kay Coughlin, director of stewardship, Oberlin College (Oberlin, OH), has worked with Memorable Miniatures, Akron, OH, to produce miniature portraits of campus buildings. The portraits include a message on back that in part reads, "....recognizing Oberlin's most generous philanthropists."

"The execution of these portraits is excellent and the production quality is quite high," Coughlin says. "It is a great value for the dollar. We have used these for our largest donors and they are a hit."

Handcrafted Artwork: Doug Draut, director of leadership gifts, Centre College (Danville, KY), says they utilize the internationally known glass artist/instructor of their glassblowing program to create unique pieces for each campaign executive committee member. "These were very well received and are collector's items," he says. "It made the thank you very distinctive and exclusive."

Sources: Therese O'Malley, Director, Benefactor Relations, Northwestern Memorial Foundation, Chicago, IL. Phone (312) 926-2466. E-mail: thomalle@nmh.org
Kay Coughlin, Director of Stewardship, Oberlin College, Oberlin, OH. Phone (440) 775-8569. E-mail: Kay.Coughlin@oberlin.edu
Doug Draut, Director of Leadership Gifts, Centre College, Danville, KY. Phone (877) 678-9822. E-mail: doug.draut@centre.edu

73 Utilize Heads of Government to Recognize Achievement

Consider the office of your mayor or governor to recognize outstanding member achievement.

Used with discretion, a proclamation from a head of government can provide an impressive form of recognition. In some cases, government officials may even designate a particular day in honor of someone.

74 Give Top Donors Special Recognition

Looking for a high-impact way to celebrate your organization's top givers?

Have your CEO refer to top donors by name in a CEO Message in your organization's annual report, insiders' newsletter, magazine or external newsletter.

75 Include Member Interviews in Newsletter, Magazine

Looking for a fun way to get to know your members? Include lighthearted personal interviews with them in your membership newsletter or magazine.

Officials with the Sanibel & Captiva Islands Chamber of Commerce (Sanibel Island, FL) began including member interviews in its news magazine in 2007.

They print and distribute some 2,000 copies of the magazine every two months.

"This feature came about through one of many creative brainstorming sessions between my husband and me," says Bridgit Stone-Budd, director of marketing.

"I wanted something light and fun, but also informative for our members," Stone-Budd says. "Through research and experience, I've realized that retaining readership is fueled by two things: local interest stories and member photos. Fellow members and business owners enjoy reading about each other."

Interview subjects answer 10 questions created by Stone-Budd. She draws from a pool of questions she crafted, but, she notes, "I do use some particular ones over and over again because I get hilarious answers."

Some of her favorite questions include:

- What did you want to be when you grew up?
- Boxers or briefs?
- Do you like Spam?

To determine which member to interview, she says, "I pick different groups of members, sometimes accommodations, sometimes the board of directors, retail, restaurants, services, etc. Then I e-mail the interview questions to about 10 to 15 in the group in hopes that I can pick at least five good/juicy ones per issue."

When creating interview questions, use a mix of serious and silly questions to create a more dynamic interview.

Source: Bridgit Stone-Budd, Director of Marketing, Sanibel & Captiva Islands Chamber of Commerce, Sanibel Island, FL. Phone (239) 472-8255. Website: www.sanibel-captiva.biz

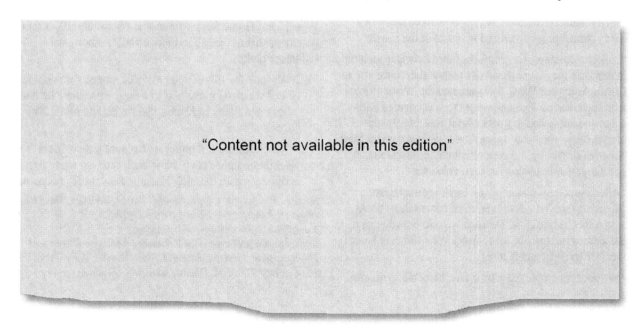

"Content not available in this edition"

76 Steward Donors Beyond the Thank You and Gift Receipt

There's more to major donor stewardship than sending thank you notes and gift receipts after donors make a gift. Reach out and make contact with them in as many ways — and as many times — as you can; and not only when they've made a gift, or to ask for another.

Here are five ways to cultivate major gift prospects beyond the standard and customary thank you and gift receipt:

1. Have your executive director and board chair personally call and thank major donors.

2. Have board members personally invite prospective major donors to programs and events.

3. Ask major donor prospects for their opinion and advice.

4. Send prospective major donors a clipping from a newspaper, magazine or website that might interest them.

5. Promptly follow up with any donor inquiries.

77 Share Major Gifts' Impact Through Newsletters, More

Whether through a newsletter, magazine or insider's report to constituents, regularly share examples of how particular gifts impact your organization. Here are ideas to get your wheels turning:

✓ Do a story about a named endowed scholarship established in the 1970s. How many students have benefited from it to date? What are some of those graduates doing today? Have any of them established similar funds at your organization?

✓ Develop an article about how a building renovation allowed you to accomplish more than anyone ever dreamed — attracting and retaining talented employees, enabling you to better fulfill your organization's mission, improving the lives of those you serve.

✓ How about an article about a program launched more than a decade ago thanks to some generous major gifts? What's happened to that program during the past 10 years? How has it helped your organization carve its reputation?

78 Surprise Your Volunteers With Fun, Positive Ideas

Do you ever surprise your volunteers to make their experience with you more fun? If so, how do you surprise them?

Amy McAden, director of volunteer services, The Kingston Hospital (Kingston, NY), offers three ideas that keep her volunteers involved and invested in the cause:

1. "I asked volunteers for pictures of themselves from a time in their life they were proud of or when they were young. During Volunteer Week, I constructed the 'Walk of Fame' with their stories. The 'today' photo was covered with a flap so people had to guess who it was. Staff were blown away when they learned one volunteer was a Miss America runner-up. I then took all the information and put it together in a book for each volunteer."

2. "After a grueling fundraiser and employee appreciation tea during hospital week, I surprised our auxiliary board with a special breakfast. The room was decorated in pink, the kitchen had baked a lot of sweet treats and each board member received a pink rose."

3. "We have an employee who is in a barbershop quartet. One day when (the quartet was at the hospital), I had them sing to the volunteers who were working. It was a really fun surprise."

Marianne Kranz, director of volunteers, Meals on Wheels and Home Support Services (Summit, NJ), offers two ideas that never fail to induce smiles among her volunteer ranks:

1. "We look for silly awards at dollar stores. One volunteer joked we always sent him to a rural area where he'd see 'lions and tigers and bears.' So we bought him a lion, tiger and bear."

2. "We collect pink flamingoes because a dear client had them on her lawn. Now each year we recognize a volunteer with the Pink Flamingo Award for teamwork."

Source: Amy McAden, Director of Volunteer Services, The Kingston Hospital, Kinston, NY. Phone (845) 334-2761.
E-mail: amcaden@kingstonhospital.org
Marianne Kranz, Director of Volunteers, Meals on Wheels and Home Support Services, Sage Eldercare, Summit, NJ.
Phone (908) 273-5554. E-mail: mkranz@sageeldercare.org

79   Recognition Ideas: VIVA Celebrates Volunteers

Recognizing volunteers with an annual awards ceremony is fulfilling for all involved. Take that gesture a step further with awards that draw special attention to volunteers' accomplishments.

The annual VIVA! (Very Important Volunteer Awards) program honors six individuals for their volunteer efforts in Delaware County (Muncie, IN).

Sara Shade, committee chair, says having a catchy title such as the VIVA! Awards is beneficial, helping community members identify with and look forward to the annual event. In Muncie, she says, the VIVA! Awards are instantly recognized.

Shade says five recipients are presented with a VIVA!, while the sixth is recognized with a Lifetime Achievement Award for displaying outstanding long-term volunteer efforts.

"The Rotary-sponsored awards have been around since 1992," says Shade. "They recognize individuals for significant contributions to cultural enrichment, education, social service, civic activities, service or fraternal organizations, or other activities within the county."

A committee of Rotary Club members from both Muncie chapters selects recipients. To qualify for a VIVA!, Shade says nominees must:

1. Live or work in Delaware County, or the impact of his/her volunteer service must be felt in Delaware County; and

2. Provide the volunteer service without expectation of financial remuneration (although reimbursement of expenses will not disqualify a nominee).

Once the nominations are made, the committee must determine who stands out among the group.

For the 2008 VIVA! Awards, recipients included a person who volunteered more than 9,100 hours over 52 years of service with a local hospital, as well as a person who spent countless hours supporting a local poverty coalition.

Source: Sara Shade, Committee Chair, VIVA! Awards, Muncie, IN. Phone (765) 289-0661. E-mail: shade@beasleylaw.com

80   How to List Names on a $1 Million-plus Donor Wall

Donors of $1 million or more deserve special recognition. Here are ways three nonprofits celebrate and honor these strong supporters of their respective institutions:

Northwestern Memorial Hospital (Chicago, IL) recognizes major donors by name on a wall of polished acrylic plates that magnetize to aluminum rails. It is tiered into sections: $1 million-$1.9 million; $2 million-$4.9 million; $5 million-$9.9 million; and $10 million-plus.

Names within each tier are alphabetized. To make it easier to add new plates or move a plate from one tier to the next, the wall has blank plates randomly interspersed among engraved plates, says Therese O'Malley, director of benefactor relations.

O'Malley says that her office runs a monthly report using Raiser's Edge software to identify any newly qualified members. "We send a recognition confirmation letter to each donor requesting their permission to list their name on the wall, as well as to confirm their recognition preference."

The University of Richmond (Richmond, VA) is preparing to reveal a new million-dollar donor wall. The wall is made of stone and the names will be engraved.

Names will be added randomly, rather than alphabetically, every few years, says Laurel Hayward, director of donor relations and stewardship.

"We sent donors a letter from the university president along with a photo of the wall and a permission sheet with a preliminary listing of their name," Hayward says. "They either signed the sheet approving the preliminary listing or made changes to it and sent it back to me."

Spouse names will be included, says Hayward, but all must be in the same format, e.g., Alice & John Smith. "We did not include degree years since we have limited space and wanted a clean, uncluttered look," she says.

Sewanee: University of the South (Sewanee, TN) has a $1.5 million donor wall as part of its Never Failing Succession of Benefactors Society. Names are listed chronologically to make it easier to update as new members join the society, says Paula Whitaker Whisenant, donor relations coordinator. The marble is cut into separate sections, making for easier removal and engraving when updates are needed.

While names are listed in a standard format (Jane & John Doe, with no degrees, titles or class years), donors are asked to sign off on the listing, she says. "We do include names of spouses, as well as foundations and businesses."

New members are recognized annually, and sometimes biannually, says Whisenant, depending on how many names they have to engrave.

Sources: Therese O'Malley, Director, Benefactor Relations, Northwestern Memorial Foundation, Chicago, IL. Phone (312) 926-2466. E-mail: thomalle@nmh.org
Laurel Hayward, Director of Donor Relations and Stewardship, University of Richmond, Richmond, VA. Phone (804) 289-8658. E-mail: lhayward@RICHMOND.EDU
Paula Whitaker Whisenant, Donor Relations Coordinator, Sewanee: University of the South, Sewanee, TN. Phone (931) 598-1632. E-mail: pwhitake@sewanee.edu

Give Thanks The Phoenix Symphony Way

When Marsha Berland, special events and volunteer manager of The Phoenix Symphony (Phoenix, AZ), prepares for the annual volunteer appreciation concert, she plans in advance. Twelve months in advance, to be exact. The event honors 500-plus volunteers in front of an auditorium filled with 2,200 guests, family members and concertgoers.

Berland shares creative ideas and techniques that help make the event a success:

- Giving each volunteer an additional ticket to invite a special guest to the concert.

- Creating a separate ticket booth labeled "Volunteer Will Call," then directing all volunteers being honored to the booth for tickets the day of the concert. Berland staffs the booth, thanking volunteers and handing out small appreciation gifts.

- Prior to the concert, presenting leaders of each volunteer group a framed letter of thanks signed by the president/CEO and the music director.

- Having the symphony marquee programmed to honor the volunteers throughout the evening, making them feel all the more special.

- After the concert, treating the volunteers to a social hour where the president/CEO and music director offer thanks for their dedication, passion, time and efforts.

Source: Marsha Berland, Special Events and Volunteer Manager, The Phoenix Symphony, Phoenix, AZ. Phone (602) 452-0424. E-mail: mberland@phoenixsymphony.org

 ## Keep Gift Challenger Informed of Matching Gifts

Let's say your organization finds a donor willing to put up a $2-million challenge gift if you can match it with an additional $1 million in gifts over a two-year period — a two-for-one match.

During that two-year period in which you are raising the $1 million, doesn't it make sense to keep the challenge donor up to date on your progress? Of course it does. That's why you should have an easy-to-read summary you can present to the donor on a quarterly basis. It keeps him/her closely involved as you are working to meet the challenge and also avoids any surprises throughout that time period.

Your report should include the challenge and matching amounts, duration of challenge (along with start and end dates), any restrictions, the names and amounts of significant gifts, stats of smaller gifts and cumulative matching gifts to date. Here's a sample design.

Challenge Gift Update

Donor:	Estelle Radeker	Challenge Amount:	$2 million
Matching Gifts Required:	$1 million	Stipulations:	None
Pledge Date:	7/15/09	Challenge Duration:	24 months
Start Date:	7/15/09	End Date:	7/15/11

Challenge Restrictions:
Challenger's gift used to establish Radeker Endowment Fund; $500,000 in matching to be added to Radeker Endowment and $500,000 in matching to support general operations for five years ($100,000 per year beginning 7/1/11).

Update for Period _____ 4/15/10

Gifts of $10,000 or more —

Donor(s)	Pledge	Total New	Cumulative
Evenrude, Harker	$25,000		
Inness, Ian/Nancy	$50,000		
Kaplan, Susan	$30,000		
Klinger, Marty/Jill	$75,000		
Lineoff, Inc.	$100,000		
Morgan & Co.	$10,000		
Stravinski, Leon	$10,000		
		$300,000	$705,000

Gifts of Less Than $1,000 —

Previous Gifts	New Gifts	New Donors	Total Donors	
$240,000	$41,000	91	214	$281,000
			Total	$986,000

83 Fulfill the Fundraising Adage: Thank Donors Seven Times

Most fundraisers know the saying that all donors should be thanked seven times or more. But what counts as a thank you? Are some forms of gratitude more valuable than others? What should a Thank-you-times-seven stewardship plan include?

"First, it's important to realize what the philosophy is behind the magic seven," says Teri Blandon, director of foundation and government development, WETA TV/FM (Arlington, VA), a public TV and radio station. "All too often, donors were being thanked profusely only once or twice — when the check was received — and then they didn't hear from the nonprofit/institution again until they received a solicitation.

"The idea behind the multiple thank yous is the essential principle of stewardship — maintain the relationship throughout the entire cycle of giving, from cultivation through solicitation, through donation, back to cultivation. And while stewarding, don't forget to thank donors for their investment in your organization."

Blandon says she thanks donors about 18 times: 12 when she sends a monthly program guide with a letter highlighting programs she thinks they may be interested in and ending with a thank you. The other five to six times include:

1. A thank-you letter when the commitment is made.

2. A thank-you letter when the check is received, with the tax reference (may be same as No. 1 if check and commitment arrive together).

3. A New Year's Eve card.

4. A cover letter with the annual report (that lists funders).

5. If they've underwritten a specific program on the station, when she reminds them of the air date and time of the program, and/or after the program has aired.

6. When she asks them for new support.

"Don't try to adhere to an artificial standard, but follow the philosophy behind it," Blandon says. "Keep your donors involved in and informed about your organization as much as is reasonably possible, and when you do have contact with your donors, say thank you."

Source: Teri Blandon, Director, Foundation & Government Development, WETA TV/FM, Arlington, VA. Phone (703) 998-2744. E-mail: TBlandon@weta.com

Make Your Seven-plus Thank Yous Count

For an expression of gratitude to count toward the seven-plus stewardship adage, it must be a personal one, says Christina L. Auch, director of major gifts, Christ School (Arden, NC).

"The annual report, while technically a thank you, usually isn't very personal," Auch says. "Birthday cards might be if they include a note from someone the donor actually knows, rather than being a general mass mailing piece."

Persons who make a major gift to the school receive a letter from the headmaster and an invitation to an annual major donor dinner, where speakers also thank them. Auch, who handwrites notes to dinner attendees with whom she has significant conversations, says: "That makes three thank yous, and if the donor is a parent, a fourth would be sent by our parent fund chair."

She shares other ways to say thank you:

✓ Ask a board member to write personal notes to major donors who give above a set level.

✓ Ask scholarship students to write a thank you to their respective donors.

✓ Ask board members to call donors and say thank you, even if it's only leaving a message on an answering machine.

✓ Ask faculty members affected by particular restricted gifts to write notes to donors.

✓ Send an article about the success of a program with a thank-you note at some point in the next several months to those donors who supported it.

✓ Invite a donor to come to a school event with a major gift officer or trustee, as their guest.

✓ Invite donors to tour a facility to which they contributed.

✓ Invite donors to have lunch with a faculty member.

Source: Christina L. Auch, Director of Major Gifts, Christ School, Arden, NC. Phone (828) 684-6232, ext. 145. E-mail: cauch@christschool.org

84 Fun Ideas to Express Your Gratitude to Valuable Volunteers

Q. In what ways do you surprise volunteers as a way of thanking them for their efforts?

"Volunteer coordinators nominate an outstanding volunteer who has served at least one year. The county mayor recognizes the volunteer in a council meeting. They receive a certificate and a clock along with a copy of the declaration that was read by the mayor. These volunteers appreciate the recognition in a very humble way."

— Virginia Lee, Volunteer Program Manager, Salt Lake County Office of Volunteer Program Services (Salt Lake City, UT)

"If I hear of a special deed a volunteer performed, I write a 'SpiritGram,' which is a recognition tool in our organization. The form describes the deed and is reviewed by several top executives in the organization. A copy is sent to the volunteer and posted on our board. As a reward, we mail them a 'free lunch' ticket for them to use in our cafeteria whenever they desire. The volunteers love the recognition and feel special."

— Cecilia Alonzo, Manager, Volunteer Services, Our Lady of the Lake Regional Medical Center (Baton Rouge, LA)

85 Appreciation Month Celebrates Members

Show your members how much you value their support with an entire month dedicated to thanking them.

Membership staff at The Children's Museum of Richmond began offering a member appreciation month in April 2005. The first celebration marked the museum's fifth year in a new building, says Stacy Smith, membership coordinator.

Since then, the annual event has grown in ways it honors members as well as in its ability to raise awareness of the museum in the region.

"We started member appreciation month as a way to show our members how much we appreciate their support and how much they mean to The Children's Museum," says Smith. "They are an essential part of our museum, and we want to show them how important they are to us."

The month-long celebration has included a raffle with prizes, such as a special delivery of cupcakes by the museum's mascot, Seymour, and an art studio visit for a small group of children.

In addition, members may bring a guest for free every day during member appreciation month, a benefit that has been very well received by members, Smith says.

Organizers are looking to further enhance the special month.

"Instead of the raffle, we are focusing on all of our members by adding more performances and activities that will happen during the appreciation month, such as our Member Monday evening program," says Smith. "This event is like a mixer where members come and socialize. It is publicized on our website and by invitation. We usually have child-friendly food, such as chicken fingers, fruit, veggies, etc. It is always held at the museum since this is an opportunity for our members to have the museum to themselves."

Cost for the special evening gathering for members varies, she says, noting that the 2007 event cost under $400.

The incentives you are able to offer members throughout an extended celebration will depend on your organization's budget. If your budget is limited, Smith suggests that offering discounts on items/programs may be more cost effective than hosting events.

Also, consider starting off with a member appreciation weekend or week if you are not sure a membership month would be feasible.

Smith says she and her co-workers ensure all members are aware of the celebration so they can take full advantage of the programs and activities that have been planned for them. "We publicize our member appreciation month on our website, in our membership brochures and mailings, and at the museum with banners and posters."

A member appreciation month is a fun way to thank your members and remind them how much you value their contributions, she adds.

"Our members have enjoyed the additional activities and events we provide for them during this month and consider it an added benefit of their membership."

Source: Stacy Smith, Membership Coordinator, The Children's Museum of Richmond, Richmond, VA. Phone (804) 474-7011. E-mail: ssmith@c-mor.org

"Content not available in this edition"

Children's Museum
OF RICHMOND

A member button (left) featuring the logo (above) of Children's Museum of Richmond (Richmond, VA) lets members share their support throughout the community.

86   Tailor Appreciation Gifts To Donors' Unique Interests

All too often, charities produce a framed photograph or certificate or purchase some other memento in mass quantities to thank donors for generous support, only to have the item end up in the donor's closet or round file.

Rather than take that approach to recognize your important donors, develop a depository of unique but not overly expensive items from which to draw for special donors.

Use this two-pronged approach to match appreciation/cultivation gifts to both prospects and donors:

1. Learn and make note of prospects' unique likes and interests early in the cultivation process. One prospect may talk about a longtime interest in matchbooks while another may mention a fondness for her English heritage. Those clues will alert you to be on the lookout for items that may not cost much but may mean a great deal to the prospect.

2. Either develop a list of unique gift items or purchase items from time to time that can be part of a depository from which to select special gifts for special persons.

Unique Gifts for Donors, Prospects

Here's a small sampling of gift ideas for major gift donors to help you develop an appropriate list of your own:

1. **Items native to your region.** For native sons and daughters who no longer live in your community, consider items unique to your city, state or region (e.g., maple syrup, regional books, a subscription to a regional magazine, a print from a local artist).

2. **Collectors' items:** Old postcards, thimbles, glassware, sports memorabilia, and more.

3. **Gifts for donors' loved ones (including pets).** Sometimes donors are even more touched by a gift directed to someone important in their lives other than themselves: grandchildren, a spouse or even a beloved pet.

4. **Difficult-to-come-by items.** Just being aware of donors' interests will help you spot a unique or hard-to-come-by item during your travels and everyday experiences — a ticket to a particular event, a gift certificate to a bed and breakfast and other such items.

---

87   Spotlight Donors Online

In addition to the traditional forms of donor recognition, more nonprofits are devoting space on their websites to recognizing top donors, knowing that recognition can lead to additional gifts while, at the same time, positively influencing would-be donors.

Need inspiration or direction on how to do so? Check out these examples of online recognition of major donors:

❑ **Clemson University (Clemson, SC)** — http://Features.clemson.edu/giving — Features 20-some photos of major donors on a single page. Visitors can click on any photo to learn the story behind each donor's gift.

❑ **Scripps Health Foundation (San Diego, CA)** — www.scripps.org/about-us_giving_testimonials — Offers a featured video of one of its principal donors.

❑ **The University of New Hampshire Foundation (Durham, NH)** — www.foundation.unh.edu/list-endowed-funds — Lists and briefly describes all of the university's named endowment funds and their donors.

---

88   Limiting Award Recipients Adds Value to Honor

 How do you recognize your most generous donors?

"(We do so) with our Texas Star Awards. The award has been in place for more than five years and honors those individuals or corporations who have demonstrated outstanding generosity and community involvement. The most recent one was given to a family foundation that made a leadership gift to The Hawks Family Foundation Wishing Place, contributed as one of the premier supporters of our Wish Night auction and had two members serve terms on our governing board.

"We don't give the award ... every year — only when there are appropriate candidates."

"We don't give the award just to give it. It is not given every year — only when there are appropriate candidates. There have only been three recipients in the chapter's history.

"(When giving donor awards), it is important to have clear guidelines for who is eligible for any award program, which helps to ensure that the review process is selective and that the award retains its value."

— *Erin Michel, Development Director-Central Region, Make-A-Wish Foundation of North Texas (Irving, TX)*

---

89   Feature Monthly Gift Profiles on Your Website

Whether you provide your constituents with a regular e-newsletter or simply encourage them to visit your website, consider featuring a monthly or quarterly online story about a recent major gift. Not only does this provide an additional way of recognizing top donors, it plants seeds in the minds of those who read about the gifts' positive impact. It opens others up to the possibilities of philanthropy.

In addition to covering both the donor and the impact of the donor's gift, your feature might include links to additional information pertaining to some aspect of your story.

---

90   Staff Step Up to Serve Thank-you Meals to Volunteers

Look for heartfelt ways to say thanks to your valuable volunteers.

At Hospice of St. Tammany (Mandeville, LA) volunteers enjoy a special treat once a year — a meal prepared by staff especially for them.

"This was a great event and very special in the eyes of the volunteers," says Sarah Ferro, office/volunteer coordinator, "because the staff did all the work.

"All of the hospice staff cooked part of the meal," Ferro says. "This year we served brisket, green bean casserole, fresh rolls, fruit salad, fresh spinach salad, garlic whipped potatoes and baked goods."

Having staff prepare the meal adds to the special feeling of the event while keeping costs to a minimum, Ferro notes.

She shares tips on how to create a similar heartfelt event to say thanks to your valuable volunteers:

- ❏ **Plan ahead to get all employees involved.** Have staff sign up to participate on a sign-up sheet that you put out at least two months prior to the event. Break the sign-up sheet into four parts: 1) starters, 2) main entrees, 3) paper products and 4) drinks. This allows staff to select what they prefer to bring and gives persons who may not be comfortable preparing food the option to bring plates, forks or napkins.

- ❏ **Send an e-mail to all employees** stating plans for the event. Emphasize the event's importance for volunteer and staff morale. The more excited you are, the more excited your staff will be!

- ❏ **The day of the event, decorate early and have plenty of places available for staff to bring food to keep it warm or cold as needed.** Have extra crock pots and ice-filled coolers on hand to preserve the food.

Source: Sarah S. Ferro, Office/Volunteer Coordinator, Hospice of St. Tammany, Mandeville, LA. Phone (985) 898-4080. E-mail: sferro@stph.org

---

91   Premiere Movie Event Offers Red-carpet Recognition

Volunteers at the LifeCare Medical Center (Roseau, MN) are treated like stars with a private showing of a newly released movie.

At volunteer movie night, Pam Sando, volunteer coordinator, shows her appreciation for volunteers by treating them to a private screening of a newly released film.

For the annual event, volunteers meet at the local theater and view a pre-selected movie for free. This year, nearly 120 junior and senior volunteers watched the exclusive viewing of "High School Musical 3," which carried a G rating, making it appropriate for volunteers of all ages.

"The volunteers loved this event," says Sando. "Some of our volunteers are elderly and don't go to movies often. This was a real treat."

Volunteers enjoyed free popcorn, soda and candy at the private showing, and could bring guests for a discounted rate.

Sando explains why a private movie screening for volunteers is such a hit:

1. The movie screening lets volunteers simply sit and relax for two hours.

2. Movie night requires very little coordination or planning and no setup or purchase of supplies, making a local movie theater the ideal location for a volunteer appreciation event.

3. The evening allowed the theater to reap the benefit of selling tickets to an existing movie for one additional day. The theater offered the medical center a discounted rate for ticket and snack pack pricing, which they purchased on behalf of the volunteers.

Source: Pam Sando and Terry Lamppa, Volunteer Coordinators, LifeCare Medical Center, Roseau, MN. Phone (218) 463-4714. E-mail: Volunteer@lifecaremc.com

---

92 Tribute Program Recognizes Caregivers, Raises $1 Million

Putting a creative twist on tribute gifts, a California healthcare system has raised more than $1 million in less than four years.

Through the Guardian Angel Tribute Program for Sharp HealthCare (San Diego, CA), a patient can honor a special caregiver by making a donation in his or her name. There is no minimum donation, and patients can honor individuals or entire departments.

"This is a way for our patients to recognize any of their caregivers — a nurse, a physician, a housekeeper — who has done something wonderful for them," says Christina Jordan, senior development officer.

Here's how the tribute program works:

- Patients in a Sharp HealthCare's hospital receive a book-mark introducing the tribute program. The bookmark, left when housekeeping staff clean a room, features the program's logo, brief description and place to write special caregivers' names.

- Four to six months after the patient's hospital stay, he or she receives a direct-mail piece that further explains the Guardian Angel program and invites patients to honor a physician, nurse or other caregiver with a donation in his or her name. Additionally, tabletop displays with donation envelopes are at each of the nurses' stations, as well as some offices.

- When gifts arrive, development staff send a thank-you to the donor within 48 hours.

- Anyone named as a guardian angel receives a letter and special lapel pin. For a person's first recognition, the patient relations director presents the letter and takes a photo of the recipient, sharing details of the patient's story when provided. Since it is common for caregivers

to receive recognition multiple times (one doctor has 81 pins), those receiving pins two through nine and 11 or more are simply sent a letter and pin. The 10th recognition earns a gold pin.

- The development staff mails the donor a second thank-you letter with a photo of the caregiver receiving his or her pin. Jordan notes that the picture taken at the initial presentation is used each time that person is honored.

- Early in the calendar year, donors receive a direct mail piece inviting them to submit a second donation in honor of their guardian angel to celebrate National Doctor's Day in March. As a gift for the physicians, the development office compiles a Doctor's Day booklet that lists guardian angels and donors who honored them.

Since implementing the tribute program four years ago, Jordan says, they have given out more than 5,300 pins to 1,577 guardian angels, with gifts in honor of the recipients exceeding $1 million. The average gift is $250 and the largest, $300,000.

Jordan credits the success of the program — which grew out of a similar, smaller-scale program in place at one of the organization's hospitals — to its simplicity and its natural fit with the The Sharp Experience, a system-wide initiative which focuses on making Sharp HealthCare the best place to work, practice medicine and receive care.

"The biggest benefit is connecting and establishing the relationship among the donor, physician and foundation," she says. "It connects those three dots."

Source: Christina Jordan, Senior Development Officer, Sharp HealthCare, San Diego, CA. Phone (858) 499-4811. E-mail: christina.jordan@sharp.com

93 Host a Reception for All Past Board Members

Many nonprofits give former board members emeritus status as a way to keep them involved after their terms end. Unfortunately, far more nonprofits do little or nothing to maintain that relationship with former board members.

If your nonprofit has let relationships with former board members slide, why not coordinate an event geared just for them? Here's how you might do that:

1. Pull together a committee made up of current and former board members, and charge them with coordinating a board appreciation event.

2. Suggest that the committee schedule an event with some

drawing card appeal — perhaps at a to-die-for home that visitors would love to visit.

3. In addition to plenty of social time, incorporate a brief program that brings past board members up to speed on your nonprofit's current happenings. In fact, you might want to ask these former board members if they would like the group to continue on a more formal basis, perhaps meeting twice a year or quarterly.

If the group of former board members agrees to form a more official capacity, you may want to involve them in any number of fund development activities.

94 Highlight Member Achievements at One-stop Shop

Set up a simple one-stop shop online to showcase member accomplishments.

In 2006, the Soap and Detergent Association (SDA) of Washington, D.C., launched "Sustainability Central" (www.cleaning101.com/sustainability) to highlight work of member companies in sustainability practices, says Brian Sansoni, vice president, communication and membership. With growing interest in environmental responsibility, many SDA members have begun including separate reports on their company websites to address consumer questions and concerns related to green issues.

In a related action, Sansoni says, the SDA board approved The Soap and Detergent Association Principles for Sustainable Development.

The document is like a three-legged stool that upholds the integrity of the organization and its members, Sansoni says, by focusing on three key areas: human health/environment; as well as both the social and economic sustainability through the responsible formulation, production and sale of cleaning products and ingredients.

The Sustainability Central website feature showcases examples of how member companies are acting responsibly in those three areas — a great, tangible benefit for members,

Sansoni says. Another benefit to the online information is that it's available to members and consumers 24 hours a day, seven days a week.

SDA keeps the website center simple to keep up to date.

"We send e-mails to our member companies' leadership, asking for any updates on their sustainability practices," he says. Members send website links to their latest activities posted online. SDA staff then put a headline and link at Sustainability Center.

"This isn't rocket science; it's easy to maintain," Sansoni says. "We didn't want to make this difficult. There are examples of sustainability practices from A to Z."

Members are allowed to showcase up to three items at a time, with the website updated monthly. "We don't want the website to be too cumbersome. We want to keep it fresh," Sansoni says. He notes that the site will continue to evolve as member needs and the nature of the soap and detergent field dictate.

Members offer positive feedback on the project, he says, noting that it also has spawned more members to produce and share written sustainability statements.

Source: Brian Sansoni, Vice President, Communication and Membership, The Soap and Detergent Association, Washington, D.C. Phone (202) 662-2517. E-mail: bsansoni@cleaning101.com

 95 Say Thanks With a Picnic

Thanking volunteers is an important part of your management role.

When Corrine Cooper, volunteer services manager, Harvesters Community Food Network (Kansas City, MO), and the organization's Americorps team want to thank volunteers, they plan a picnic.

They choose a theme (this year's: Volunteers are Sunsational) for a simple idea that makes a lasting impression.

Cooper offers easy, inexpensive tips for hosting a volunteer thank-you picnic:

- Ask donors to contribute items for prizes and gift bags.

- Send e-mail invitations to reduce print and postage costs.

- Check storage closets for items with your organization's logo to add to gift bags.

- Seek a major gift donation for a raffle. Cooper scored a flat screen television as the big drawing item at the picnic.

- Hold the picnic indoors, preferably with outdoor access as well so the event can be held rain or shine.

- Hang beach towels from a clothesline strung across the room as decorations. In the corner of the room, place a large beach umbrella, under it place the gift bags and raffle items.

- Go to the local party supply store for inexpensive extras like beach balls that you can blow up and place around the room to add color.

- To follow the sunsational theme, ask everyone to wear flip flops, Bermuda shorts and Hawaiian shirts.

- Play music that boosts the beach theme such as the Beach Boys.

- Give each guest a door prize such as mini-sunscreen or bags of sunflower seeds with handwritten thank-yous.

- Have an executive of the organization or a local celebrity speak to show the extra level of appreciation.

- Most importantly, have staff from the organization help set up, serve and mingle with the volunteers.

Source: Corrine Cooper, Volunteer Services Manager, Kansas City, MO. Phone (816) 929-3057. E-mail: CCooper@Harvesters.org

96 Add Element of Surprise to Awards Presentations

Want to make your volunteer awards event even more special for top recipients? Here's an idea that deserves consideration:

When your top volunteer steps up to be recognized, have one of the most important persons in the volunteer's life surprise the recipient by walking into the room unannounced. You could even have this key person hold a plaque, ribboned medallion, statue or other symbol of the award recognition and make a formal presentation.

Whether the presenter/surprise guest you enlist is the recipient's spouse, son, daughter, parent, mentor, college professor, best friend or other key person, everyone at your event will enjoy the amazement your special volunteer experiences as he/she sees this special person arrive. The excitement will help make the awards presentation memorable not just for the recipient, but for everyone privileged to be witnessing it.

97 RSVPs Ensure Seamless Volunteer Recognition Event

Knowing how many volunteers and guests to expect at your volunteer recognition event can allow you to properly plan this important celebration.

A registration form doubled as an RSVP form for the volunteer recognition event for the Arthritis Foundation Eastern Pennsylvania Chapter (Pennsylvania, PA), helping organizers know how many attendees and attendees' guests to expect at the March 2010 breakfast buffet/awards ceremony.

Of the nearly 1,300 volunteers invited, more than 210 returned RSVPs.

"We want our recognition events to have a fun and energetic feel to match the personalities of our spectacular volunteers," says Wade Balmer, director of operations and mission integration. "This is an event to pump volunteers up, honor them and show them how much we appreciate their volunteerism. The event isn't long — it's on a Saturday from 10 a.m. to 12 noon. (The Pennsylvania suburb of) King of Prussia is chosen as the location because it's easy to find, accessible via public transportation and several major roads and people can make a day of it and shop at the mall afterwards."

Balmer says that because each volunteer is presented with a certificate of appreciation at the recognition event, asking volunteers to RSVP assisted planners in preparing certificates in advance. RSVPs also afforded event planners the opportunity to gauge attendance and prepare the appropriate amount of food for the group.

Balmer adds that the written RSVP registrations have generated interest from persons beyond the organization's volunteer base, allowing the organization to reach out to these people to offer them opportunities to volunteer and/or give to the cause.

Source: Wade Balmer, Director of Operations and Mission Integration, Arthritis Foundation-Eastern Pennsylvania Chapter, Philadelphia, PA. Phone (215) 971-5476. E-mail: wbalmer@arthritis.org. Website: www.arthritis.org

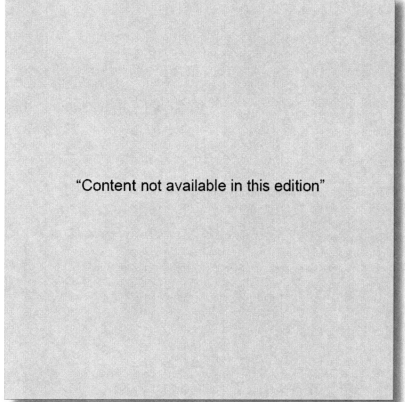

"Content not available in this edition"

This RSVP form, included in the event flyer and online, helped organizers of a volunteer recognition event for the Arthritis Foundation-Eastern Pennsylvania Chapter (Philadelphia, PA) better plan by informing them who would be attending, and if they would bring guests.

98 Recognize Top Corporate Donors in Special Ways

Major donors deserve major praise.

Corporate donors at one university receive traditional recognition — listing in internal publications, online articles and naming opportunities. But for the top 100 corporate donors, school officials go a step further, listing them in an advertisement in the local newspaper and statewide business weekly.

This additional publicity also helps to raise awareness of the corporate program within the business community.

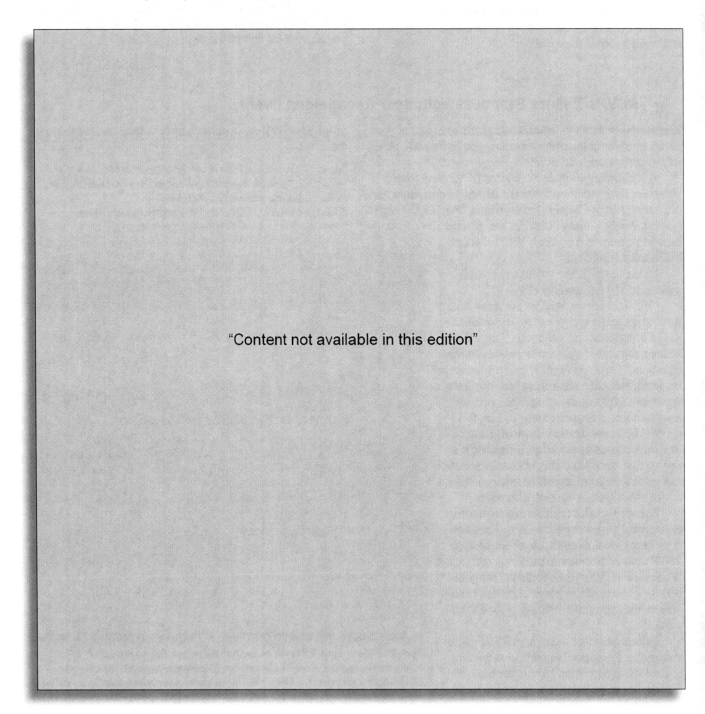

"Content not available in this edition"

100 Celebrate Your Members With Monthly Birthday Parties

If most of your members are within a short drive of your organization's headquarters, celebrate their birthdays and give them an opportunity to mingle with one another with a monthly party.

Staff with the Center for Active Generations (Sioux Falls, SD) have hosted monthly birthday parties for members for more than 25 years, says Lisa Howard, program director.

"This is just one way we can say thank you and honor our members," Howard says. "People like to feel special and enjoy getting together with others to celebrate. It's a no-brainer for a membership organization to acknowledge these special days."

Offered the second Friday of every month, the parties begin at 2 p.m. and last an hour to an hour and a half. They are free to attend, and are held in the center's dining room. Attendance ranges from 130 to 180 persons, including members and their guests.

All members, not just those celebrating a birthday that month, are invited to the monthly parties. The center holds a new-member social the hour before the birthday parties to encourage new members to attend popular monthly events.

Members celebrating a birthday that month are announced at each party and given a special name tag to wear.

Center staff publicize the parties through its website and monthly newspaper/program guide. The newspaper/guide includes pictures from the previous month's party, names of all members celebrating a birthday that month and credits the party sponsor.

The birthday party is sponsored by the Good Samaritan Communities of Sioux Falls. The organization provides the birthday cake and provides each birthday guest with a special cookie baked by the organization's nutrition department.

"It's a no-brainer for a membership organization to acknowledge these special days."

Party attendees have a chance to win door prizes, which include two $50 gift cards for a regional supermarket chain that are good for groceries or gas. All attendees' names are placed in a box to be drawn for the door prize.

A volunteer master of ceremonies and other volunteers serve the cake and check guests in at the door.

For entertainment, the parties typically feature chorus groups and drama clubs from local schools that perform for no charge.

Howard offers this advice to other member organizations thinking of hosting monthly birthday parties: "Keep it simple and keep it fun. Great entertainment is a plus and fun door prizes make the event attractive to members and guests. Also, keep the event at about an hour and a half."

Source: Lisa Howard, Program Director, The Center for Active Generations, Sioux Falls, SD. Phone (605) 336-6722. E-mail: LHoward@cfag.org

101 How Do You Acknowledge Anonymous Gifts?

John Carroll University (University Heights, OH) recently received a $4.45 million anonymous bequest — the largest anonymous gift by an individual in the university's 124-year history — to support scholarships.

"We spent some time with the donor to understand why she didn't want to be named and then determined what we could do to recognize the gift commitment that would respect her wishes," says Doreen Knapp Riley, vice president for advancement.

They chose to use a press release to announce the anonymous gift, along with a small thank-you dinner with the donor's family, university president and board chair. The donor saw and approved the press release before it was sent out and was also told where and when it would be sent, says Riley.

"The donor understands the value of philanthropy and how announcing the gift and its purpose, in the form of a press release, might encourage others to give scholarship gifts," she says.

The donor was also involved in selecting the date, time and place of the thank-you dinner, as well as who would be invited, says Riley. "We sat down with her and discussed, 'This is what we are planning, what do you think?' to make sure that she was comfortable with everything."

At the dinner the person most respected by the donor will acknowledge the gift and the donor's commitment to the institution, she says.

The donor's anonymity is respected at every step, says Riley. For instance:

✓ Very few people know the identity of the donor.

✓ Very little information is included in the donor's record.

✓ A code is used in place of the donor's name in the gift file and only two people know where the file is located.

✓ The president and board chair acknowledge the gift.

"Every donor is unique and wants to be acknowledged in a different way," says Riley. "When it comes to donor recognition and stewardship, we want to do whatever the donor is comfortable with and is appropriate for the university."

Source: Doreen Knapp Riley, Vice President for University Advancement, John Carroll University, University Heights, OH. Phone (216) 397-4345. E-mail: driley@jcu.edu

102 ## Celebrate Staff Victories Each and Every Month

To help keep development staff energized, make a point to celebrate achievements on a regular basis. To that end, consider creating recognition awards that may even include inexpensive but meaningful incentives such as a bonus day of vacation, designated parking spot or a gift certificate to a local restaurant.

For example, issue staff awards for:

- Most calls completed in a month.
- Most creative fundraising approach.
- Largest gift closed in past month.
- Most dollars raised in a month.
- Most upgraded gifts in the month.
- Most first-time gifts in a month.
- Best stewardship actions in the month.

103 ## Combine Volunteer Appreciation With Education

The Lakes of Missouri Volunteer Program (LMVP), Columbia, MO, combines volunteer appreciation with education. In April 2009, LMVP staff organized a volunteer appreciation event that included speakers and presentations in an effort to promote volunteer education in addition to acknowledging the efforts of their ever-important volunteers.

Tony Thorpe, LMVP's volunteer coordinator, answers questions about the event:

How many volunteers do you have? How many attended the volunteer appreciation event?

"We have about 100 to 150 volunteers in our group. While we have 80 to 100 active volunteers with training, there are many more people who accompany our volunteers and assist. We're a statewide program, with volunteers spread out all over the state. At our volunteer appreciation event we hosted about 30 people, traveling from up to 250 miles away."

In what ways did you show appreciation to volunteers at the event?

"We give fleece pullovers to volunteers who have been with the program for five years.... Our 10-year volunteers receive binoculars.... We gave a husband and wife team who clocked 15 years a handheld GPS unit. We also purchased a few things and got a few others donated to hand out as door prizes. We tried to get a few nice items rather than a bunch of throwaway things. After every couple of presentations we'd break for snacks and coffee, then use the door prizes to get folks back to their seats. It worked very well!"

What educational offerings were held at the event?

"We arranged for presentations, just like a conference. We had presenters from state and federal resource agencies speak on invasive species, fisheries and aquatic plants — a total of three presentations — a college professor talked about the influence of land use on water quality, a 12-year LMVP volunteer who works with a lake board talked about his experiences controlling inputs from the watershed, and the Lake of the Ozarks Watershed Alliance executive director gave a talk. University of Missouri (home of the LMVP) professor Jack Jones spoke during dessert. LMVP staff gave a few talks throughout the day concerning LMVP data, using the data for developing nutrient criteria and reservoir hydrol-

ogy. We wrapped up with an interactive session regarding where the volunteers want to take LMVP."

What advice do you have for combining appreciation and education at volunteer events?

1. **"Involve volunteers in the planning of the event.** This was an amazing help! I handpicked a group of volunteers from across the state to assist in event planning. We had a sit-down lunch meeting one day and ironed out what types of presentations they wanted to hear, where we should have the meeting (important for a statewide project), how to best spend our budget, etc. I was amazed at how much more science these folks were hungry for. I had completely underestimated their ability to digest hard science. So, that leads us to the next point:

2. **"Don't underestimate the volunteers when planning the educational component.** As stated above, I wasn't prepared for how eager the volunteers would be to learn the hard stuff. In the planning phase we asked the volunteers what types of talks they wanted to hear and what questions they'd like to have answered by the speakers. They came up with some complex questions! We summarized their questions and gave them to the presenters early on so the presentations could be tailored to the event.

3. **"Start planning sooner rather than later.** Buildings may fill up and caterers might get booked before you can get to them, but even more importantly the volunteers' calendars fill up quickly. Many of our volunteers are retired and I am always surprised at how busy retired people are! They are filling their calendars up several months in advance, and if you're not on there early, you get left behind!

4. **"Give them breaks during the event.** Whether to go to the bathroom or just get the circulation going in their legs, people need a break. And be sure to offer guests drinks and snacks, too. You'll find them gathering near the food talking to one another and making connections."

Source: Tony Thorpe, Coordinator, Lakes of Missouri Volunteer Program, University of Missouri, Columbia, MO.
Phone (800) 895-2260. E-mail: tony@lmvp.org.
Website: www.lmvp.org

104 Donor Recognition Idea

Your organization received a $15 million gift to renovate a building from the child for whom the building was named. How do you recognize the donation?

Since holding the event at the building itself or doing the customary ground-breaking isn't practical, consider hosting a dinner at which you display photos of the original building side by side with artists' renderings of planned renovations. This will provide an eye-catching display while showing the donor how his/her gift will benefit your organization.

As a memento to the donor, consider framing a print of the original building.

105 Volunteer Bulletin Boards Help to Recognize, Recruit

Create a volunteer bulletin board in a high traffic area of your facility. Use it to:

✓ Post photos of new volunteers and shots of volunteers in action.

✓ List volunteer accomplishments.

✓ Include a photo and profile of your volunteer of the week (or month).

✓ Include a wish list of needs that have yet to be met through volunteer assistance.

✓ Post a calendar of upcoming events.

106 Four Ways to Express Heartfelt Appreciation on a Budget

When it's time to pay special tribute to someone highly important to your organization, remember that some of the most meaningful gifts of appreciation are those that require creativity, time and input from a variety of people, but not necessarily a lot of cash.

Chances are the person you are honoring already has a wall filled with plaques, inscribed crystal paperweights and engraved silver bowls. Rather than looking to add to this collection, seek instead a way to create a more meaningful form of recognition.

Here are ideas to get you started on your personalized recognition:

Make a 'This is Your Life' Video

Create and produce an amateur video of your honoree's life featuring highlights of involvement in your organization. Interview friends, volunteers, administrators, board members and others whose lives have been touched in a positive way. Show results of projects the honoree has helped complete and the impact those projects have had on persons your organization serves. Include video of photos of the honoree in a candid moment, or working with others — but let the honoree believe it's for another purpose until you are ready to screen your production.

Create a Commemorative Work of Art

If you have a skilled artist among your volunteer base, ask the person to draw a portrait of the honoree as part of a collage spotlighting his or her accomplishments for your organization. Invest in quality framing so the recipient will be proud to display it.

Or you may wish to create a simpler but equally heartfelt project. Gather young artists (children you serve, or children of your staff or volunteers) to paint a large mural to present to your honored supporter. You also can ask them to paint individual works following a theme, then assemble and present the works in a large bound book.

Another idea: Engage talented adult volunteers to create a group project, such as a set of holiday ornaments, hand-painted glassware or beautiful needlepoint. If they sew, each could create a square for a colorful quilt.

Make a Memory Book

Buy a large, well-made scrapbook (with room for additional pages) and fill with photos and mementos such as event programs, ribbons, badges, news clippings and special items to provide a timeline of your honoree's involvement. Ask friends and family to help locate photos.

Chances are several of your volunteers are quite skilled at scrapbooking and would be happy to create a multi-paged work of art for your honoree using the many themed stickers, picture anchors and creative papers available.

Ask everyone in your organization who knows the honoree to sign the book, and even write messages of congratulations and appreciation, high-school yearbook-style.

Give Special Donors Their Own Special Day

Make a proclamation to hold an annual Pat Johnson Day at your institution on a date that is important to your honoree. Have your chief executive officer, board members and other appropriate officials and even your mayor sign the certificate. To add even more meaning, mark that special day as an annual date for your institution to do something meaningful in the recipient's honor, like begin an annual campaign, host a luncheon or start a canned food drive.

107 Personalize Member Gifts, Incentives, Rewards

Many member organizations give out renewal rewards, anniversary gifts or other perks to their members. If you do so, consider personalizing gifts based on member suggestions.

Include a question on member applications and member surveys that asks them to list specific gifts or rewards that they would like to receive (see sample, at right).

Make it clear that you are just asking for suggestions so that your members do not feel disappointed if they suggest "jewelry store gift certificate" and do not receive one. For example, state: "We are looking for suggestions to reward you, our all-important members, for your loyalty. Please share your three favorite ideas for gifts that you as a member would enjoy receiving."

Ask them to be specific. For example, say: "Please name the establishment(s) from which you would like to receive a gift certificate."

Record answers in a database to which you can refer when deciding on gifts or rewards to give members.

The responses will help you better serve your members while providing insight into their likes and dislikes.

How Can We Say Thanks?

At XYZ Organization, we're constantly looking for ways we can better serve you, our valuable members. To help us in that area, we'd like your input on possible ideas we can say thanks.

Your name: _____

Your e-mail: _____

Please check any/all items that you as a member would enjoy receiving as a thank-you gift:

- ❑ Gift certificate to (be specific): _____
- ❑ One free guitar or singing lesson
- ❑ A free massage at a local salon
- ❑ Free session with dog walker or pet sitter
- ❑ Tickets to a film or comedy show
- ❑ A bottle of your favorite wine
- ❑ Other: _____

We appreciate your input as we strive to improve our member services. To learn more about membership benefits, please call us at (555) 555-5555 or visit us at (Web address).

Please mail this questionnaire with your membership renewal form or fax to (555) 555-5556. Thank you!

---

108 Choose Five Simple Ways To Recognize a Member

Representatives of membership organizations know that retaining members is a critical key to the success of the organization. And sometimes, the simple gestures can be the most meaningful.

Try these simple suggestions in making your members feel special:

1. Acknowledge the member's birthday with a call or a card.

2. Feature a member in each issue of your newsletter, emphasizing his/her specific, unique contributions to the organization. Consider a question-and-answer format for an easy read, along with a flattering photo.

3. Invite the member to speak at an upcoming meeting.

4. Create space on your website or at your office/facility for members to share thoughts and ideas.

5. Make a goodwill phone call totally unconnected to upgrading membership or any other business of the organization. Simply call and ask the member if there's anything the organization can do for him/her and say, "Thanks for being a member."

---

109 Acknowledge Donors In Unique Ways

Q. **What unique ways are you acknowledging your planned giving donors?**

"One of the member benefits for our Benedictine Legacy Society is a Saint John's Estate Planning Binder. This binder has an embossed cover showing our Abbey Church, a major architectural touch point. It has plastic sleeves for holding documents related to a donor's estate plans, such as trust documents, will, advisor's contact information, etc. Each section has a log for noting the latest information additions.

"Some donors use it as the basic storage for their papers and keep it in a secure location. Others put photocopies of documents in the sleeves with notes describing the location of the original documents. We very strongly recommend that originals be placed in safety deposit boxes or other secure locations.

"Many donors have expressed appreciation for the usefulness of the book in two ways: It reminds them of what documents are important and also provides a copy of the documents for heirs to use to identify originals."

— *Jim Dwyer, Director of Planned Giving, Saint John's University and Abbey (Collegeville, MN)*

110 Thank-you Calling Campaign Involves, Inspires and Educates Board Members

Board members at SHALVA (Chicago, IL) — a nonprofit that provides domestic violence counseling services to the Jewish community — regularly call donors to say thanks.

"I think it is impossible to thank donors too much for supporting SHALVA's programs, especially given the current fundraising environment," says Ava Newbart, director of development. "These simple thank-you calls are a great opportunity for SHALVA to personally connect with donors. They are also a way to inspire our board to keep fundraising and promoting SHALVA to our community."

Since SHALVA's office has only four phone lines and a small budget, Newbart asks board members to call donors on their own.

For their first calling campaign, board members called all year-end donors of $50 or more. Newbart e-mailed board members a script, call report form and a list of names with phone numbers. Each board member was asked to make an average of 20 phone calls, for a total of approximately 400 calls.

Newbart followed up with board members via e-mail, encouraging them to make their calls and send her back the forms. "One board member e-mailed me back and asked, 'You want me to call, say thank-you and not ask for anything else? Are you sure?'" she says. "I reassured her, and other board members, that their phone calls would be well-received and that they would be happily surprised at donors' responses."

She also reminds board members that with the economy as it is, SHALVA must reach out and personally contact donors; that it's much easier to keep current donors than to find new donors; and that the need for SHALVA's services is on the rise.

For other nonprofits considering starting a simple thank-you campaign, Newbart advises: "Just do it and keep it simple. Being a one-woman shop is challenging. We've talked about making personal thank-you calls for a long time, but there were always competing priorities. Given the climate, our board was open to trying new strategies. Keeping our donors happy is an agency-wide mantra."

Source: Ava Newbart, Director of Development, SHALVA, Chicago, IL. Phone (773) 583-4673. E-mail: anewbart@shalvaonline.org

Two tools that staff with SHALVA (Chicago, IL) provide to board members to make donor thank-you calls are the call report, below, and informational sheet with sample scripts, at right.

"Content not available in this edition"

The Conversation:
The intention of your call is ONLY to thank donors for their gifts received.

Sample Opener:
"Hello, Mr./Mrs. X. My name is Jane Brown and I'm a member of the volunteer board of directors of SHALVA. I am calling to thank you for your support of our organization. We received your recent gift and I wanted to let you know, personally, how very much we appreciate it."

At this point, simply pause and wait for a response. Some donors are quite startled and don't know what to say. Usually, they are very appreciative and gracious.

Most calls are very short, simply ending after you express your thanks. **Please do NOT make any comment that could be construed as another request,** such as "We are grateful for your gift and hope you will continue to support us in the future." This hints of another solicitation, and we want to avoid leaving that impression.

Sample Closer:
You can end the call by simply wishing the donor a pleasant evening.

Sometimes a caller will ask you about how SHALVA is doing or will want some information about our programs and services. If you are comfortable answering their questions, by all means do so. If not, perhaps you could ask if they would like a staff member to contact them separately. If so, please let us know. If a donor expresses an interest in giving more or in volunteering time, you can definitely engage in that discussion. Other organizations' experience with thank-you calls by board members has shown that a small number of donors want to discuss making an additional gift and sometimes it can be significantly higher than the gift they have recently made.

What happens as a result of these calls?
Donors who receive a personal call (including those who received messages left on answering machines) will be specially coded by the office, and any additional information gathered during the calls will also be recorded.

The next time these donors are solicited along with other donors who did not receive a call, we will be able to compare their average gift levels, their rate of response, the promptness of response and other information. We can continue to compare these groups for a couple of years, which will allow us to measure long-term loyalty of the two groups. Though we anticipate that donors who receive personal calls are likely to show greater loyalty over time and make increasingly generous gifts, we need reliable information from this test for future planning and forecasting.

Recognize the Efforts of Long-distance Members

While recognizing the efforts of members who may be assisting you from far-off locations is important to retaining them, doing that can be challenging.

Make time to create a menu of recognition strategies for these more distant members. Examples may include:

- A lapel pin or piece of jewelry that designates their special relationship to your organization.
- Scheduled phone calls to discuss business and unscheduled calls to pat them on the back.
- Posting information on your website noting their valuable contributions.
- Sending a card and personal note during unexpected times.

- Insider news that regularly lets them know they're appreciated.
- Thank-you phone calls from higher-ups (board members, CEO, others).
- Publishing their names as VIMs (very important members).
- Placing an ad in their local newspaper that publicly recognizes them.
- Sending an occasional photo of events taking place at your organization.
- Mass-producing and sharing a DVD of a special event or ceremony.

 Feature Donor/Gift Profiles

Regularly include donor gift profiles in each issue of your constituency newsletter or magazine as well as on your website. Doing so is a great way to publicly recognize the generosity of major donors and also serves to plant the seeds of philanthropy in others' minds on an ongoing basis.

Although it's important to focus on the donor and what motivated him/her to contribute, it's even more important to give ink to the impact that the gift is having or will have on your organization and those it serves.

Donor profiles also help to improve readership of your publications and website. People enjoy reading about others' gifts — how they came about, why the donor decided to fund a particular project and how that gift is making a difference.

Use these communications venues to shine a spotlight on ways donors have made gifts to illustrate the possibilities available: gifts of property, gifts of stock, annuities and more.

 Personalize Post-event Volunteer Notes of Thanks

When wrapping up a fundraising event, don't forget one important detail — tell your volunteers thank you!

The Food Bank for Larimer County (Fort Collins, CO) hosts four signature fundraisers each year, each requiring the assistance of approximately 100 volunteers. Once an event wraps, volunteers receive a personalized thank-you note with specific details about how their contribution truly made a difference.

Charlene Olms, volunteer and development coordinator, sends a letter to each volunteer after every event stating how much was raised in total, how much the silent auction raised and a personalized note specific to that event.

Olms says organizers of one of this year's fundraisers met with an unusual challenge when several volunteers fell ill and others had to pick up the slack. Olms was sure to mention this in her thank-you note and recognized those who stepped in to cover with a gift certificate for an ice cream treat.

Olms also includes her e-mail address in the thank-you note asking the volunteers to contact her with their ideas and suggestions for event success in the future.

When sending a personalized thank-you note, follow these tips:

- Handwrite the note whenever possible for an extra personal touch.
- Note the significant contributions volunteers played at the fundraiser. Be specific. Detail amount raised at the event (or other goals achieved) and note how much was raised from each component of the night, especially where volunteers were involved, such as the silent auction.
- Mention the special ways in which volunteers went above and beyond the call of duty specific to the event.
- Add a small gift of thanks, such as a gift certificate, as a token of your appreciation.
- Include your contact information in the note so volunteers can reach you with their comments and/or suggestions about the event.

Source: Charlene Olms, Volunteer and Development Coordinator, Food Bank for Larimer County, Fort Collins, CO. Phone (970) 530-3113. E-mail: colms@foodbanklarimer.org

114 Include Donors in Post-campaign Success

Just because your capital campaign has successfully concluded doesn't mean the party's over. It's important to share your campaign's success with donors. After all, their generosity made it a success.

Involve donors in your post-campaign period in the following ways:

- Convey appreciation in a personal way through various methods: personal letters from your organization's CEO, campaign chair and others.

- Follow through on naming gifts with appropriate plaques. Check with donors to be sure names are spelled and listed correctly before authorizing the engraving.

- Invite donors to celebrate in the completion of renovated or newly constructed capital projects to which they contributed. Consider a larger, all-inclusive celebration as well as more individualized gatherings.

- For donors who establish named endowment funds, revisit the details of the fund: how annual interest will be used, the agreed-to name and fund description and such.

115 Impress Members With Personal Thank-you Cards

Contacting members with an occasional personal note builds good will and keeps them connected to your cause.

Volunteer members at Morristown Memorial Hospital (Morristown, NJ) regularly receive handwritten thank-yous for their efforts from Beth Upham, manager of volunteer services. Upham sends cards to two volunteers each week. Taking care to use their first names, "I write to them about how they make a difference," she says. "They love it."

Upham uses a spreadsheet to track notes to her 1,125 volunteers. She also keeps an index card for each volunteer, placing it in the volunteer's file.

To add an even more personal tone, Upham routinely asks volunteers to indicate their favorite form of praise and reward, recording this information on the index cards. Then when she writes the notes, she refers to this information to word her message accordingly.

Source: Beth Upham, Manager of Volunteer Services, Morristown Memorial Hospital, Morristown, NJ. Phone (973) 971-5476. E-mail: beth.upham@atlantichealth.org

116 Wrap-up Newsletter Honors Event Volunteers

Creating an event newsletter is an unusual and supportive way to thank volunteers for donating their time and efforts that helped carry out the successful event.

Here's a design for a simple four-page newsletter, filled primarily with photos, that will engage volunteers and give them a stronger sense of accomplishment after the event is complete:

✓ *Page 1:* Create an overview of the event, including details of its success. Recap the event by adding the goals developed at the beginning of the planning stage, amount raised, if applicable, and number of volunteers who participated before, during and after the event. Add photos of volunteers in action as they were preparing for the event and during the event.

✓ *Page 2:* Create a page that shows who this event helps. If your event raises funds for a specific need in your organization, be sure to describe that need on this page and include photos of those the event helps. If the event raises money for your general fund, include photos or detailed information as to how your organization will use the proceeds.

✓ *Page 3:* Include a list of items donated and sponsors who participated at the event. Not only does this boost the volunteer efforts, it creates a catalog of who your donors and sponsors were so that you can call on them the following year.

✓ *Page 4:* Use the entire last page to offers thanks and kudos to all involved. Create a list of volunteers who participated in the event and a list of those who donated to and sponsored the event. Carefully check this page to ensure that all names are spelled correctly and that everyone who helped is included.

✓ *Voilà!* The newsletter is done! It now becomes the thank you that you can send to all volunteers, sponsors and donors of your event. Not only have you created a chronicle of your event that will be a useful tool for the following year, all involved will appreciate the effort put into this piece and will be more willing to participate in the same event next year.

117 Ask Employees to Help Steward Donors

Donors appreciate hearing from those who benefit from their generosity.

Encourage your nonprofit's employees whose work or departments may be positively impacted by major gifts to show their appreciation to those who made it possible. Ask that employees keep your office aware of and involved in such gestures of appreciation so as not to be left out of the communication loop.

118 Give Thought to Volunteer Award Names

Rather than simply presenting an outstanding volunteer award, why not put some thought into these special awards?

Officials with Mercy Medical Center (Des Moines, IA) named one of their volunteer awards the Catherine McCauley Award in honor of McCauley, an advocate for the poor in Dublin and founder of the Sisters of Mercy.

Putting some thought into the names of your volunteer awards makes them more meaningful and prestigious for those receiving them.

119 Develop a Menu of Stewardship Actions

You may find it helpful to develop a menu of stewardship actions tailored to first-time donors. Such a list may include (but not be limited to):

____ Special thank-you letter from CEO.

____ Special thank-you letter from board chair.

____ Orientation, get-acquainted sessions for new members.

____ Welcome packet of information.

____ Periodic updates on use/impact of first-time gift.

____ Personal visit from the CEO.

____ Invitation(s) to serve on a committee.

____ Facilities tour.

____ Event/reception invitations.

____ One-on-one review of strategic plans report.

____ Induction ceremony into special gifts club.

____ Lapel pin or some other official membership designation.

____ Introductions to others associated with your organization (e.g., employees, board members, other major donors).

Having a menu of stewardship actions for these first-time donors — and evaluating what's taken place and what's planned — will ensure that members of this special group become longtime friends and supporters of your cause.

120 Awards and Rewards Help Recruit and Retain Members

An awards program can serve to reward your existing members and garner attention to grow your membership base.

Staff at Associate Builders and Contractors, Inc. (ABC) headquartered in Arlington, VA, know the importance of recruiting and retaining members. To encourage recruitment and retention among members in its 78 chapters with a combined membership of more than 24,000 firms, staff developed an awards program offering incentives to members through the Beam Club.

Under the Beam Club, first established in 1966, ABC members are recognized for their commitment to grow the association by rewarding them with valuable gifts.

"ABC National supports the membership recruitment efforts of our chapters with our Beam Club program which recognizes members for their efforts," says Doug Curtis, vice president of chapter services. "We purchase and provide the awards so the chapters may recognize and reward members for their efforts. The awards are presented by the chapters."

Each member recruited is worth one point with points accruing year to year, advancing the member chapter to the next award level within the program. A member sponsor is enrolled in the Beam Club once five members are recruited.

Once 50 new members are recruited, the member receives national recognition by reaching the Beam Club Hall of Fame, with his/her name placed on the Hall of Fame plaque and chapter profiled in ABC's weekly electronic newsletter.

Club awards include plaques, lapel pins, shirts, jackets, watches, mantel clocks and more.

Source: Doug Curtis, Vice President of Chapter Services, Associate Builders and Contractors, Inc., Arlington, VA. Phone (703) 812-2009. E-mail: curtis@abc.org. Website: www.abc.org

121 Allow Donors to Share In Accomplishments

Whether you are completing a successful capital campaign or simply working at landing more major gifts, it's important for donors to share in your organization's accomplishments. After all, it's their major investments that make possible some of your organization's most impressive achievements.

Be sure your donors are aware of and take ownership in each of your organization's accomplishments. If it's impossible to see each of your donors face-to-face, craft a personalized letter signed by your CEO or board chair that delineates major accomplishments during the past year or so. Send it to those who generously gave of their resources and give them the credit they deserve for those accomplishments.

The sample letter shown here helps to illustrate how an accomplishments letter might be constructed.

Dear Jack and Ellen:

This has been a remarkable year for Emerson Boys and Girls Home. In fact, thanks to friends such as you, it's been a transformational year. Because of your generosity, our agency has established a regional reputation that is attracting immeasurable positive attention.

Allow me to give a partial rundown of what's been happening at Emerson thanks to you and others:

✓ Completion of a $3.5 million expansion allowing us to serve an ever-growing population of young people who desperately need our services.

✓ The addition of $750,000 to Emerson's endowment which will allow us to not only maintain our past level of services but enhance them even more.

✓ The most positive certification review Emerson has ever received in its 52-year history.

✓ A significantly increased success rate of improved academic standing among former clients.

✓ An annual membership that has grown by 31 percent in the past 24 months.

✓ The addition of more talented, highly skilled personnel.

I could go on, but you get the picture. And don't for one minute think that you didn't play a role in all of this. You did! And we value your partnership very much.

Dr. Erik Erikson said, "Children love and want to be loved and they very much prefer the joy of accomplishment to the triumph of hateful failure." Those of us who make up the Emerson family — you among them — also prefer the joy of accomplishment. Thank you for continuing to make that joy possible.

Sincerely,

122 Tell Volunteers Thanks a Latté!

When Becca Wexler, volunteer coordinator, Village Shalom, Inc. (Overland Park, KS) wants to thank her volunteers, she says, "Thanks a latté!"

More than 150 volunteers were invited to a Starbucks coffee tasting organized as a show of appreciation for their service to the retirement community. A Starbucks barista conducted a presentation on coffee types, flavors, aromas and the best food pairings to have with each type of coffee.

Here are a few tips for hosting your own volunteer appreciation coffee tasting:

❑ Decorate tables with a coffee theme. Wexler used greens, browns and creams as coordinating table colors and sprinkled tables with coffee beans.

❑ Create invitations with a coffee theme. The Thanks a Latté! invitation had a picture of a steaming cup of coffee on the front. Wexler ordered invitations from VistaPrint (www.vistaprint.com), an online source she says offers quality invitations at a reasonable cost.

❑ Consider time of day. While the Thanks a Latté! event was in the evening, planners have decided it may be

more successful held in the morning since guests will be trying caffeinated coffees.

❑ Encourage volunteer participation with giveaway opportunities. Each volunteer attending the event received a coffee mug, and volunteers were entered into a contest to win coffee gift cards and other prizes.

❑ Use giveaways as part of your decor. Wexler used an earthy and decorative mug, plate and bowl set as centerpieces on the tables and played CDs from the local coffee house that were later used as prizes for guests.

❑ Purchase items in bulk. Coffee beans for the event came from Sam's Club.

"Thanks a Latté was a fun and creative approach to recognizing our volunteers," says Wexler. "The volunteers were introduced to various Starbucks roasts as they got to know each other over a rich cup of coffee."

Source: Becca Wexler, Volunteer Coordinator, Village Shalom, Inc., Overland Park, KS. Phone (913) 266-8310. E-mail: bwexler@villageshalom.org

123 Appreciation Event Celebrates Volunteer Accomplishments

Each year 2,000 volunteers lend a hand at Meals on Wheels Greenville County (Greenville, SC). The organization says thanks with an annual volunteer appreciation event.

The most recent event, titled 2009 Breakfast of Champions — Everyday People, Extraordinary Accomplishments, featured "The Biggest Loser" contestant Amy Parham, who spoke of great things ordinary people can accomplish with determination and hard work.

"There are so many heroes — fireman, soldiers, policemen, doctors and unsung heroes like our volunteers, everyday people who do extraordinary things," says Jan Dewar, director of volunteer services, in explaining the event's theme.

Dewar shares her tips for hosting a successful volunteer appreciation event:

✓ Host an appreciation breakfast to allow for the most volunteers to attend.

✓ Draw a well-known, inspirational speaker. Find out who within your organization knows someone willing to address your volunteers. Think outside the box to determine who within your community could address volunteers in an inspirational way.

✓ Organize a committee led by a passionate employee who will put in the time to create an appreciation event that relays how important volunteers are. Shelley DiMarco, food service manager, headed up Meals on Wheels' most recent event, overseeing a committee that solicited door prizes.

✓ Provide items for volunteers to take home. Attendees of the Meals on Wheels event received a canvas bag, bottled water, hand sanitizer and a pen.

Source: Jan Dewar, Director of Volunteer Services, Meals on Wheels Greenville County, Greenville, SC. Phone (864) 233-6565. E-mail: janice@mowgvl.org. Website: www.mealsonwheelsgreenville.org

---

124 List All Endowment Funds In Honor Roll of Contributors

If you publish an annual honor roll of contributors for those on your mailing list, be sure to include a section that lists all endowment funds, even those to which no one contributed during that fiscal year. List the endowment fund in bold and those who contributed to that endowment fund immediately beneath it.

Those who contributed to a particular endowment will receive the recognition they deserve and endowment funds that received no contributions for that fiscal year will send a subtle message for others to make a contribution in the new fiscal year.

Endowed Funds —

Melissa and John Weinberg Endowment Fund
• Melissa and John Weinberg

Elston Macke Endowment Fund

Robert Houston Endowment Fund
• Sharon Houston
• Martin Houston
• Townsend Plumbing

---

125 Donor Recognition Idea

Looking for a creative way to share the impact of a major gift with the donor who made it all happen? LaShon Anthony, small business consultant with visuals4 (Chicago, IL), shares an out-of-this-world method: Name a star after the donor.

This opportunity is available through the International Star Registry (Ingleside, IL). Learn more at http://starregistry.com.

Source: LaShon Anthony, Small Business Consultant, visuals4, Chicago, IL. E-mail: info@visuals4u.com. Website: http://visuals4u.com

---

126 Ask Volunteers How They Want to Be Recognized

Put out a suggestion box for recognition ideas. Ask volunteers to submit and sign ideas on how they personally would like to be recognized. You many not be able to fulfill everyone's wish, but will surely get an idea of what appeals to them.

127 14 Ways to Recognize Major Donors

As an organization, it is vital to recognize the donors and their gifts. How do you do that?

1. Hold an annual major donor recognition event.

2. Create a major donor giving society.

3. Host a luncheon or breakfast event that honors select major donors.

4. List major donors' names by giving level on a special recognition page on your website.

5. Profile major donors in your print newsletter and/or website.

6. Create a donor wall in your lobby that recognizes donors by giving level.

7. Invite major donors to special dinners hosted by the CEO, board of trustees.

8. Offer behind-the-scenes tours.

9. Introduce major donors to those who lead the projects or programs they are funding.

10. Send donors a hand-signed acknowledgement letter and follow up with a personal phone call from the executive director or CEO.

11. Send a press release announcing the gift, making sure the donor's local media receives a copy.

12. Hold pre-event parties exclusively for major donors.

13. Offer free admission tickets and/or event tickets to major donors.

14. Provide up-to-date insider information in the form of a print or electronic newsletter or through personalized mailings to individuals.

128 Stewardship Protocol

Are you publicizing major gifts — and their impact — on your website? If so, keep in mind that many people, particularly senior citizens, are less familiar with this medium and may not have the advantage of viewing your site.

Whenever you make mention of a donor's gift on your website, do one of two things:

1. Sit down with the donor and show him/her the story that talks about the gift; or,

2. Print out the website story and send or deliver it to the donor with an explanation.

No one deserves to see your website story more than the donor who made it all possible.

Lightning Source UK Ltd.
Milton Keynes UK
UKOW01f0752060813

214894UK00007B/320/P